Strange Facts
About Death

Strange facts about Death

Webb Garrison

ILLUSTRATED BY CHARLES COX

Abingdon   Nashville

Strange Facts About Death

Library of Congress Cataloging in Publication Data
GARRISON, WEBB B
    Strange facts about death.

    Bibliography: p.
    Includes index.
    1. Death—Miscellanea. II. Title.
BD444.G28   128'.5   77-12230

ISBN 0-687-3994-0

MANUFACTURED BY THE PARTHENON PRESS AT
NASHVILLE, TENNESSEE, UNITED STATES OF AMERICA

To
Countless Numbers of Persons
Who Wonder

Preface

Measured by any standard, death is the most absorbing of the many passages to which humans are subject.

Among cultures and during epochs that have little else in common, kings and common folk alike have been almost inordinately concerned with the end of life in the body—plus the hazards, adventures, journeys, and triumphs of the disembodied spirit, or soul.

Only for a few generations in modern times has there been widespread reticence to think about and talk about final things. Largely, perhaps, through impact of new issues, plus a resurgence of interest in the paranormal and a flurry of personal testimonials about out-of-body experiences of persons pronounced clinically dead, modern Americans have suddenly rediscovered that death and dying are valid topics for thought and conversation.

Combining lore plus folklore, this volume comes to focus upon what may seem queer, odd, absurd, fascinating, or even humorous aspects of this universally absorbing aspect of life. It has not been written simply to impart information but also to entertain!

Webb Garrison

Contents

Strange Facts
About Death

Funeral Preparations and Customs

NO SYMBOLS, NO RITES

General Zachary Taylor, twelfth president of the United States, occupied the White House only a little more than a year. He died there on July 9, 1850. Commissary General J. P. Taylor, his brother, promptly claimed the body and refused suggestions that it lie in state for admirers to file by as a final tribute.

Probably (but not positively) in conformity with wishes expressed earlier by Zachary Taylor, his body was moved by fast horses to the Taylor family cemetery, now located in metropolitan Louisville, Kentucky. No one dressed in black or wore mourning bands. No traditional funeral music was played. There was no funeral; and no religious rites were conducted at the graveside.

Committed to the earth totally without ceremony, the resting place of Taylor's body is marked by a simple monument inscribed only with one of his own frequently expressed sentiments: "My only regret is for the friends I leave behind me."

TWENTY-THREE REHEARSALS

In total contrast to Zachary Taylor, Colorado farmer Jim Gernhart wanted a funeral "with all the trimmings." What's more, he was willing to do all he could to be sure that every

13

word and each gesture would be just right. "I don't want to be buried like a dog," Gernhart frequently said.

Beginning in 1951 he held a rehearsal of his own funeral once a year. Just one of them, the first, cost him more than $15,000. For it, Gernhart rented the armory in Burlington, Colorado, brought in a minister from Kansas, bought a lavish display of flowers, and provided a good meal for an estimated one thousand "mourners."

For twenty-three years, until shortly before his death at age ninety-seven, Gernhart rehearsed his own funeral—though never again in the lavish style of 1951. Unexpected publicity generated by the many funeral services for one man caused the prosperous ex-farmer to become locally noted as "the living corpse." At first he tried to shed the nickname, but after it had clung to him through numerous funerals, he admitted that he "sorta liked to be the only living corpse in the entire U.S.A."

EXACT INSTRUCTIONS FROM FDR

Few persons have gone to the trouble and expense of rehearsing their funerals; countless numbers of persons—from ordinary folk to world-prominent leaders—have left more or less precise directions about what they want done when they receive their last tribute.

Franklin D. Roosevelt would never have picked up a book of this sort. He positively loathed the word *death* and avoided talking about it. Only under extreme pressure would he put his feelings aside and attend the funeral of a person very close to him or a dignitary to whose memory he owed honor.

Yet, it was FDR, of all persons, who left the most explicit set of instructions about his funeral to be penned by a president of the United States. Diametrically opposed to the

14   STRANGE FACTS ABOUT DEATH

views of Zachary Taylor (who gave no hint that he wanted even the simplest of rites), Roosevelt in 1937 prepared a handwritten directive for his own funeral.

This remarkable document indicated (to the minute) how long the funeral service itself should last. It specified the precise time at which a special train bearing his coffin should leave Washington. Attendance at last rites was to be limited to immediate relatives, with only two representatives from each house of Congress, plus three reporters and an equal number of cameramen. FDR gave directions concerning the height, width, and length of his tombstone and even indicated the direction in which it should face.

When he died, a few of his specific instructions were given token obedience; but, for the most part, national leaders and close relatives alike agreed to ignore the written directives of the only man ever elected to four terms as leader of his nation.

MOURNERS OUTWITTED NAZIS

Early in October, 1943, a somber procession slowly moved through the streets of Copenhagen, Denmark. Members of the German army of occupation gave mourners no more than a passing glance; they had been notified that the destination was a cemetery on the grounds of Bispebjerg Hospital.

Clearly, no Nazi officer noticed that of the approximately two hundred persons who made up the procession which moved solemnly into the cemetery none returned to the city streets when ceremonies were over.

Dr. Karl Koster, registrar of the hospital, had conceived a stratagem that he hoped might save a few of the city's Jews. From the graveside, they went in small groups into scattered buildings of the hospital. From that haven, they were smuggled out of the country.

At least a dozen solemn funeral processions, including

more than two thousand "mourners," filed past alert Nazis without incident. Jews who made up the various processions were disguised briefly as patients, hidden in nurses' quarters, or "admitted into the psychiatric ward." As long as they stayed, they were fed from the hospital kitchen.

Some later left the hospital on foot by night. Most were taken in heavily loaded hospital ambulances to the city's wharves where they boarded fishing vessels in order to get out of Denmark with their lives. Eventually discovered by the Gestapo, the underground railroad whose first depot was a graveside was forced to stop operating—but not before it rescued an unprecedented number of marked persons, including Dr. Koster himself.

THE PIONEER LENT FOR LINCOLN'S USE

Reared in a log cabin, Abraham Lincoln had one of the most elaborate funerals of modern times. Many notables wanted him buried in Washington, but his widow insisted that he must be laid to rest in Springfield, Illinois.

As a result, after Lincoln's body had lain in state and services had been conducted in the nation's capital, a special funeral train was organized. Instead of proceeding directly from Washington to Springfield, the train made a leisurely circuit that permitted stops in several major cities.

As the train approached Chicago, Lincoln's widow made still another demand. Her dead husband's body must ride from Chicago to Springfield, she insisted, in an elaborate new sleeping car built not long before by George Mortimer Pullman.

Harrassed officials agreed to Mary Todd Lincoln's demand before they realized that Pullman's car had been little used because it was too big for most railroads of the era. Constructed at the cost of $18,000, the rolling palace that

Pullman had dubbed *The Pioneer* was a marvel of engineering but a financial failure. Since it was twelve inches wider than ordinary cars and stood fully two and one-half feet higher than most, it couldn't pass under bridges or through tunnels with ease.

For the dead emancipator, officials of the Chicago & Alton Railroad were willing to do anything. They sent crews to cut platforms, widen bridges, and make other changes so that, with Lincoln's body riding in grand style, *The Pioneer* could get to Springfield from Chicago.

TRIAL RUN

In preparation for the funeral of John F. Kennedy, the body of the martyred president was placed in an enormous metal casket. A special handpicked casket team of eight military men was selected to carry the coffin up the thirty-six steps

FUNERAL PREPARATIONS AND CUSTOMS   17

into the Capitol rotunda where the body would lie in state before burial.

Men who made up the casket team were taken aback to discover that they could hardly walk with their burden. They laid it on the black-draped catafalque, used earlier to support the coffin of Abraham Lincoln, then went into an emergency huddle.

That evening, November 24, 1963, the officer in charge ordered the heaviest available casket from Fort Meyer. Completely filled with sandbags, it was hauled to the Tomb of the Unknown Soldier. There, in the moonlight, an officer and a sentry perched on the lid of the coffin to increase its weight while the eight-man casket team marched up and down the darkened steps so there would be no danger of stumbling under their burden the next day while watched by U.S. leaders plus dignitaries from 102 foreign countries.

FUNERAL BLACK

Black as the mandatory color to be worn at funerals and during periods of mourning has lost its grip upon modern America. As late as the 1860s, however, relatives and friends wouldn't have thought of appearing at a funeral in any other color. Many persons wore black from head to toe, then draped black trappings on horses that drew the hearse. So much black was required for these purposes that big mercantile shops stocked a special bolt of cloth, called "funeral black" and claimed to be distinguishable from other kinds of black cloth.

In addition to relatives of the deceased, the director of the funeral procession and his special aides, or lictors, wore black. Like many other customs linked with death, the use of black at funerals was borrowed directly from ancient Romans.

Romans, in turn, borrowed the custom from far older cultures where the dread of spirits of the dead was general and pervasive. Black, considered a color of respect during many centuries, won its place in funeral processions because it was widely thought that a person dressed in black wouldn't be recognized by the ghost of the deceased.

Though predominant in many lands for many epochs, black has never been the universal color of mourning. Chinese long preferred purple; Burmese leaned toward yellow; and Ethiopians preferred grayish brown.

Flaunting then-universal European customs, King Henry VIII of England wore white during his period of mourning for Anne Boleyn. Detractors later said the color signified that he would mourn only briefly.

COST-CUTTING COMPROMISE

Mourning bands are seldom seen in the United States today except in neighborhoods of big cities where large numbers of Americans of various ethnic backgrounds are concentrated.

Typically—but not universally—a black mourning band is worn slightly above the left elbow. Wearing it gained acceptance not as a special tribute to the dead but as a cost-cutting compromise.

Families with many members and households with great numbers of servants found long-traditional black garb for funerals increasingly expensive. A woman's mourning outfit complete with veil was seldom past usefulness before it, or the man's equivalent, was replaced by everyday clothing.

Especially in Germany and in England, it became customary to require servants and retainers to wear black gloves plus black crepe around their sleeves in lieu of black from head to toe. Once these symbolic garments became commonplace, relatives began to use them too.

FUNERAL PREPARATIONS AND CUSTOMS   19

Mourning bands never entirely displaced black apparel, for persons of wealth often clung to the traditional and costly custom of wearing nothing but black when attending a funeral or observing a time of mourning. But among ordinary folk, bands gained rapidly in popularity because they were inexpensive.

PROPER MUSIC FOR THE MARCH

Composing special music to be used during a funeral procession has been virtually a worldwide practice. Until modern times, tempo of music (no matter whether it was to be played upon tribal drums or fifes and cornets) was determined by human gait. Composers in many lands fitted their somber tunes to the artificially slow pace of mourners.

In major cities of Europe, importance of "great music for great Persons on the way to the grave" was taken so seriously that funeral marches occupied part of the talents of composers like Ludwig van Beethoven, Georg Friedrich Händel, and Frederic Chopin.

Though it is not well suited for use during a ride to a graveside in motor vehicles going twenty miles an hour, the most popular of modern funeral marches (still widely used when services are held in cathedrals) comes from Chopin's opus 35. The solemn music is not a melody to which slow-walking mourners may easily adjust their pace but a musical tribute to the "death" of Poland when that nation lost its independence.

WELL DRESSED FOR THE JOURNEY

Clothing made especially for the purpose is often used to dress the dead. In rural Rumania, for example, an elaborate "death shirt" is often ordered years in advance by both males and females. Some who cannot afford such a special article of clothing put aside the attire worn at the time of marriage, so that it will be unspoiled at the time of death.

A standard service offered by many Western mortuary establishments is a line of new garments for the period of lying in state. In lieu of purchasing these increasingly expensive accessories, many relatives select the newest and best suit or dress belonging to the deceased.

Present-day motives for dressing a corpse in the best possible clothing are clearly mixed. Survivors are consciously or unconsciously eager to make a good impression on friends. Lingering sometimes far below the conscious level, however, there is the worldwide belief that a dead person should be well dressed for the final journey.

This concept is so deeply rooted that attempts of burial reform societies to give good clothing to the needy living and to dress the dead in simple shrouds have met with stubborn resistance.

"THE OLD MAN DIED"

A familiar American song about grandfather's clock tells a story in poetic fashion. According to the song, there was a mystical affinity between the clock and its owner. At the precise instant that the timepiece ceased to tick the spirit of its owner slipped from his body. Much earlier views about death and time provided the foundation for the modern song.

For practical purposes, death brings time (not just hours and minutes but also days and years) to an end. But spirits are not always aware that death has taken place and that time no longer matters. Both to speed the spirit of the dead on its way and to protect the living from danger that a spirit will linger in familiar haunts, it became customary to stop clocks (and later watches) when death occurred.

Absence of the ever-present ticking sound of early mechanical timepieces was considered to be an important signal; it helped to notify a spirit that it couldn't remain in or near the body and should take off for far places immediately if not sooner. Because clocks and watches were deliberately stopped as close to the instant of death as possible, popular thought conjured up the idea of a mystical bond by which death itself stopped clocks; or the last tick of a treasured clock was a signal for the angel of death to come claim the soul of the clock's owner.

HARDEST OF HUMAN BONES

Because teeth are by far the hardest of human bones, they have played a prominent role in modern archaeology. Even when bones have rotted and the skull has turned into dust, teeth may remain relatively intact for tens of thousands of years.

Extraction was practiced at least as early as the time of the Egyptians, who built some of the world's most awesome tombs and monuments. These people and many others customarily retrieved from the dentist any and all extracted teeth so that they could be buried with the rest of the body.

During centuries when bones and other relics of the dead were widely used in medicine and in magic, teeth from a dead man's skull were especially prized. Two or three of them (placed in a bag with the foot of a mole and hung by the chimney) were considered effective in protecting whole families from the discomfort of toothache.

"Preventive dentistry" of this sort eventually gave way to new and radical ways of putting the hardest of human bones to work. False teeth carved from ivory (or in the case of George Washington from wood) or other substances didn't last long when fixed in jaws of the living.

STRANGE FACTS ABOUT DEATH

Pioneer American dentist Levi S. Parmly, whose work brought him international fame during the nineteenth century, discovered how to secure really hard replacement teeth. With his brother, he spent days at the site of the 1814 Battle of Bridgewater and joyfully reported that he collected "thousands of teeth, extracted from bodies, of all ages, that have fallen in battle." Many of these relics of war were used to fashion dentures that Parmly correctly guaranteed to "last a lifetime."

LIGHT ALONG THE PATHWAY

Perpetual lights burn at the grave of John F. Kennedy, at the spot that tradition labels as marking the tomb of Christ in the Church of the Holy Sepulcher, and in many other places linked with death and burial. Many Orthodox Jews are scrupulous to burn a lamp for twenty-four hours every year at the time the anniversary of a loved one's death is observed. On All Souls' Day, faithful Catholics light votive candles for the departed.

These and many other ritualistic uses of candles, lamps, and torches are survivors (often greatly modified from original practices) from periods when it was felt that a spirit newly liberated from the body needed light to aid it on the dark journey to the great beyond.

In many instances, light served to help the living as well as the dead; for fire, in any form, was considered to be effective in discouraging evil spirits who might be tempted to take possession of a body recently emptied of its spirit.

Still almost universally linked with death and dying, ceremonies and customs that employ candles are as diverse as human nature. In the Scottish lowlands, the oldest survivor of a dead person waves a lighted candle over the corpse three times, then sprinkles it with salt. Unwritten laws of rural Rumania stipulate that a close relative of the deceased pass over the grave a lighted candle and a pinch of salt, along with a jug of water, a towel, and a black hen. In many parts of South America, a community is considered to be threatened with disaster unless a lighted candle is placed in the hand of every corpse. Even in the most modern U.S. funeral parlors, lights burn all night in any chapel where a corpse lies.

BELL RINGERS WELL PAID

During many centuries one item of expense for survivors was the fee that must be paid for the ringing of the soul bell. Every cathedral and church of medieval Christendom had such a bell, almost always the largest one in the bell tower.

By the time John Donne wrote the immortal line "for whom the bell tolls," ringing of the soul bell—in a distinctive pattern, or knell—was popularly taken to be merely a public notice that a death had occurred. This use of the soul bell came into importance relatively late, however.

Not simply in Christian Europe but also among primitive tribes and highly developed non-Christian cultures of the Orient, bells have been linked with death. Notes from bells (rung in special fashion) served to help convince a spirit that there was no need to remain close to a useless dead body. At the same time, noise made by bells was considered to be especially effective in driving away the evil spirits who prowled about hoping to seize a newly released soul or to put obstacles in its path.

Ringing of the soul (or passing) bell was long considered so vital that bell ringers demanded, and got, big fees for using it. Still in general use by the British as late as the era of King Charles II in the seventeenth century, bell ringers then regulated the number of strokes of the passing bell so that the general public could determine the age, sex, and social status of the deceased.

BEESWAX FOR FINEST EFFIGIES

According to many systems of thought, every soul is eager to be remembered in vivid detail. Lacking a tangible guarantee that its memory will remain fresh, a soul may be reluctant to depart from the land of the living.

Hence, it has been widely customary to fashion little figures, or effigies, showing as well as possible the actual features of the dead. Wood, cloth, and even straw have been employed in the manufacture of these memorial figures. Long ago, however, craftsmen discovered that the finest effigies require pure beeswax, which lends itself to skillful sculpture and retains its shape for years when given proper care.

A small oratory above Islip chapel in Westminster Chapel, London, long served as a storage place for beeswax effigies of the great. Usually dressed in fine or regal clothing, these little figures were sometimes set up in cathedrals or churches as temporary monuments while stonecutters did their work. At least in England, complimentary poems and epitaphs were often attached to an effigy with pins or paste.

In China, it was customary to make carefully shaped effigies of wheat flour or of soft paper, since beeswax was scarce and costly. Instead of three-dimensional effigies, Tibetan mourners settled for "face paper" printed with a figure representing the deceased. Regardless of the material used or the degree of skill displayed by craftsmen, typical death images were considered effective in convincing souls that they would be remembered so need not hang around.

SINS CONSUMED BY EATING

Every person has committed some sins against the religious system to which he belongs; some have committed many sins. Small sins as well as big ones serve as encumbrances to the spirit of the dead. So runs the system of thought that produced one of Christendom's most colorful agents: the sin-eater.

Rooted partly in scriptural references (see Hos. 4:8; Lev. 16), the practice of aiding the dead by ritualistic eating of their sins persisted in rural Britain until modern times. Many villages had a semiofficial sin-eater (nearly always a male).

When death struck, relatives sent for the sin-eater and arranged for him to sit at the door of the death chamber during the wake. As pallbearers bore the corpse toward the grave, the sin-eater took bread, cheese, and beer from the chest of the corpse, where it had been placed by a close relative. By consuming the food that had been close to the heart of the dead, the sin-eater was considered to free the spirit of the dead from the weight of sin.

Independently of Christian beliefs and rites, Hindus of ancient India devised their own method of reducing or eliminating a dead person's burden of sin. As death approached, Brahmins made random choice of a scapegoat from among the relatives. This person stepped to the side of the dying person, publicly announced willingness to accept the transferral of sins, then accepted a gift of coins from the person whose burden was lifted, or from his relatives.

Burial cakes baked by early Dutch settlers in the New World, marked with initials of the deceased and eaten at funerals by relatives, were adapted from the earlier custom of formal sin-eating.

SPIRIT MARRIED TO A FIR TREE

An adult male who dies or is killed before having taken a wife is regarded as among the most restless of spirits by farm folk of Rumania, who developed and have perpetuated one of the world's strangest funeral rites.

Among them, the long-sacred fir tree plays a prominent part in wedding celebrations.

At the death of an unmarried adult male, young men of the community go into the forest and select a well-shaped fir about thirty feet tall. Felled by hand, woodsmen alternate with the ax in such a fashion that no man takes more than one stroke at a turn.

As the symbolic tree is brought into the village, women and girls come to meet it singing the "Song of the Fir Tree." While other preparations for the funeral proceed, girls decorate the tree with ribbons and fragments of feminine clothing.

As part of the ceremony of interment, the trunk of the tree is planted at the head of the grave where it remains for months before rotting. Words of the "Song of the Fir Tree" repeated at the cemetery make it clear that the tree is a symbolic substitute bride whose role is to console the lonesome spirit of the man who is buried.

To make certain that the dead man's spirit will not fail to understand the symbolism of the tree, in many districts it is common for groomsmen and bridesmaids (dressed in traditional wedding attire) to march in the funeral procession.

CARRYING OUT DEATH

As practiced for centuries in many parts of eastern Europe, the community-wide ceremony of carrying out death for the

sake of the living came to center upon a personified Death
that symbolized all the dead.

Instead of making an effigy of an individual corpse,
villagers used straw to portray Death. Sometimes they put
the figure on a pole and carried it to a nearby town where
they paraded through the streets, singing. After singers
received refreshments from townsfolk, it was customary
either to take Death into a field and burn him or to throw him
into a swift-flowing stream.

When more elaborate preparations were made to rid a
place of all spirits of the dead in a single ceremony, a puppet
was likely to be used instead of a straw effigy. Strict
community customs dictated that a male puppet representing Death should ride on a pole carried by a girl or woman,
while a female figure of Death had to be transported by a
male. Such ceremonies were often conducted during Lent.

A variant, long common in Silesia, involved ritualistic
destruction of a symbolic figure of Death by a party of girls

and women who sang about their intention of burying Death under an oak tree so that he would depart from their village and never come back.

PROTECTION AGAINST THE EVIL EYE

Already very old when the early Hebrew scriptures were committed to writing (see Gen. 46:4), the practice of closing the eyes of the dead emerged out of concern for the living. Many specific ideas developed about the common theme according to which any person seen by the eye of a corpse is threatened with some type of danger or curse brought about by the evil eye. Frequently it was believed that anyone who came within the field of vision of a dead person was thereby doomed to follow soon that person to the grave.

The custom of forcibly closing the eyes of the dead is worldwide. To keep lids closed until rigor mortis set in, it was often necessary to use small weights. More often than any other objects in common use, coins served in this role. Their prominence here may have been augmented by age-old concepts according to which the living were to provide the dead with coins so that the toll exacted for crossing into the next world could be promptly paid.

CROWN OF VICTORY

Circular funeral wreaths, rapidly being displaced by floral offerings of other shapes, stem from practices among the Greeks and the Romans. They used wreaths (preferably of laurel) with which to crown victorious military leaders, famous athletes, and even kings and emperors. Symbolic use of greenery was a much older custom, as indicated by the role of the olive leaf in the biblical story of Noah and the flood.

Ancient Egyptians maintained special flower gardens in

which they produced greenery plus blossoms with which to crown their dead. Among them, flowers had more than merely symbolic meaning. They served as colorful and sweet-smelling sacrifices to the dead, presented to the dead with the hope that these sacrifices would make them so content in the spirit world that they would not return to the land of the living.

Because use of the funeral wreath was clearly and deeply rooted in pagan beliefs and practices, early Christian leaders did their best to put it to an end. Religious prohibitions had little if any effect. Instead of waning with the rise of the commercial florist, the practice of sending floral offerings at the time of death has greatly increased in modern times. Ancient notions about keeping spirits of the dead happy have generally been forgotten, and flowers clustered in some form of vase generally greatly outnumber round wreaths flanked about a casket.

Even in the United States, however, where persons have stopped growing their own flowers and depend upon commercial sources, many a friend or relative still stipulates use of the round wreath that so long symbolized victory.

HAND OF GLORY

Revival of black magic and other occult practices in the space age underscores virtually universal human yearning for mastery of hidden power. Unlike physicians who sought such mastery for the sake of healing, witches and other practitioners of black arts had as their goal the control of evil or demonic power. One widely used device that has figured in many rites and ceremonies was the dead man's candle, or the Hand of Glory.

For such a ghoulish charm, the preferred instrument was the right hand of an executed criminal. But in celebrated

STRANGE FACTS ABOUT DEATH

witch trials of 1610, Juan de Echelar said that since no felon's hand was available, he made a Hand of Glory from the arm of a child who had been strangled before baptism.

Regardless of source, the Hand of Glory was first mummified, then bleached. While appropriate incantations were uttered, the seeker for demonic power used virgin wax, Lapland sesame, and fat from a hanged murderer to mold a candle. This taper was placed in the mummified and bleached hand, prepared in advance, so that when the candle was lighted it would become a Hand of Glory.

Professional burglars paid high prices for such torches on the theory that the ghastly light would enable them to go about their work unseen. As late as 1831, Irish thieves captured in the act of ransacking a mansion in County Meath were found to be using a hand of glory as their only source of illumination.

DEATH MASKS

Effigies that represented the dead, in literal or in symbolic style, have been popular among many "primitive" peoples. Only in highly developed civilizations have the living found ways to create masks that represent (in actual size) the features of the dead.

Nearly always prepared as tokens of respect and emblems of mourning for the great, such masks (like effigies) probably had their origin in eagerness to please spirits of the dead. Egyptian masks, often made of gold, were designed actually to portray those in whose memory they were made.

Centuries later, development of new materials for use by artists and sculptors (notably, plaster of Paris) created an enormous demand for masks actually formed by pressing a suitable substance against the features of a corpse. Napoleon's death mask, made of plaster, created such interest that a public subscription was raised for reproduction of the work executed on St. Helena within hours after the emperor's death.

Madame Tussaud's waxworks in London—most famous in the world—got its start through the work of an artisan who at first specialized in death masks. A young woman made masks of many persons executed during the French Revolution. Later, as a refugee in England, she started shaping wax models of heads instead of plaster masks, or negative molds.

Development of photography and improvements in that art generally made the death mask obsolete; a photograph was quicker, not nearly so messy, and was far more lifelike than negative impressions made with plaster of Paris. In Russia, many graves bear photos of occupants.

BEE CUSTOMS

With the possible exception of the silkworm, no other insect has been linked with human welfare so long and so intimately as the bee. Honey was the only available sweetening agent until comparatively modern times; in order to get the precious stuff, bees were domesticated before the beginning of written history.

Since the bees were so closely linked with humans during so many centuries, widespread superstition held that the spirit of any dead person (but especially the spirit of a beekeeper) could take the prized insects with him into the great beyond.

As late as the eighteenth century, a special precaution was taken at the time of a death in rural England. A close relative of the deceased knocked on the beehive and solemnly informed insects that a death had occurred, with ceremonial repetition of the dead person's name serving as notice to bees

that they should not follow that person. In Devonshire, an additional precaution was taken. At the moment a corpse was carried from the house, any beehives he had tended were carefully turned around.

CEREMONIAL TRIBUTE RETRIEVED

At the midpoint of the nineteenth century, rites that had flourished among the ancients were still respected. Few except the very wealthy had jewels or gold to bury with their dead, but even the poorest were accustomed to placing a handkerchief or a thimble or a pocket knife in the coffin as a final tribute.

Painter-poet Dante Gabriel Rossetti wanted to let relatives and friends know the extent of his grief when his wife of two years died from tuberculosis. He pondered various grave gifts, eventually decided that the finest thing

he could bestow on her was a manuscript volume of his own poetry.

Duly buried with all the proper ceremonies, Elizabeth Siddal Rossetti took with her to the great beyond her husband's poems—lying between her cheek and her auburn hair.

As years passed and grief began to wane a bit, the poet had second thoughts. He persuaded friends to risk fines and imprisonment by digging up the body of his beloved—and retrieving the verses he had given to her "forever." Rossetti put the water-soaked volume into the hands of a "medical man" with a request that it be carefully dried, leaf by leaf. The physician did his work so well that when published the poems that had literally come from the grave were not fragments, but complete works that won quick literary success.

Burial

IMPROVING ON NATURE

Formed chiefly by action of water spanning many centuries, natural caves used as burial places suggested a logical next step: tombs hand cut from rock, with either more or less care and cost.

Where sandstone is abundant, as in the Near East, rock-cut tombs abound. Many of them were produced in the late Stone Age and the early Iron Age, when tools were scarce and costly. Once techniques of stonecutting were perfected, simplicity gave way to grandeur that could have been produced only by incredible expenditures of time and effort.

At Jericho it became customary to cut shafts into soft stone, then to create artificial caverns at the ends of shafts. A typical hewn chamber, perhaps four feet high and fifteen feet wide, might be cut from rock for the body of a single chieftain or for the remains of forty or fifty ordinary persons. Usually (but not always) bodies were reverently placed in niches or on shelves, without any type of container for the corpse.

Architecture of the rock-cut tomb became increasingly elaborate as iron tools became more common and versatile. At Petra, the Nabataeans cut from native sandstone great tombs adorned with columns, doors, and niches. As a final touch, many of these tombs were decorated with ornate pieces of sculpture fashioned from rock that was quarried on the spot.

"EARTH TO EARTH"

"Earth to earth, ashes to ashes, dust to dust" gained prominence as a modern verbal formula used in Christian burial through impact of the *Book of Common Prayer* of the Church of England. There, the familiar phrase continued, "in sure and certain hope of the Resurrection unto eternal life."

Though far from universal, burial in the earth has been practiced in almost all parts of the world. Because bodies placed in the ground deteriorate relatively rapidly, archaeologists have no way of knowing whether earth burial preceded cave burial or followed it.

At least as early as the time of the great Greek scholar Plutarch (46?–A.D. 120?), it was proverbial that placing a body in a grave had deep symbolic meaning: "Earth back to earth, the soul on high."

Some scholars believe that the very practice of earth burial stemmed from prehistoric religious views. It was Mother Earth from which all flesh came; hence it was logical to consign the body (but not the spirit) of the dead to her embrace. This view has left a lasting imprint upon burial customs of India, where the formula for interment is still likely to be, "Go into kindly mother earth, who will be wool-soft like a maiden."

Such ideas are so clearly pagan in origin that medieval Christians made a strong effort to modify age-old language. Especially among peasants, there was so tenacious a tendency to use inherited formulas that in 1904 the king of Saxony forbade by edict, use of the standard and popular

German tombstone inscription "Hier ruht im Mutterschoss der Erde" ("Here rests in Earth's maternal womb").

GOD'S BLAZING SERVANT

Burial, mummification, and other methods of handling the dead are at least partly aimed at preservation (for a short or a long time) of the body. This is not so with cremation.

Burning of dead bodies was common in some parts of Europe during the late Stone Age. This practice spread during the Bronze Age and early Iron Age, with the result that in many parts of the world a person would have been horrified at the thought of being buried in the earth after death.

Fire, according to a common motif in many cultures, is "the blazing servant of God." It not only masters the cold of winter and serves to make foodstuffs edible; fire "can free the soul from the body and fly with it to the distant land of the dead, for quick rebirth."

Some North American Indians of Pacific Coast regions considered cremation mandatory rather than optional. According to them, "unless the body is burned the soul will never gain freedom from earth. In the hot smoke, it rises to the shining sun to rejoice in its warmth and light—then flies away to the happy land in the west."

Archaeological finds in Scandanavia indicate that at least some early north Europeans tried to aid fire in its celestial work. Burned wings of jackdaws and crows plus burned feet of crows were found mixed with bones of a young person. Wings laid on the pyre along with the body were almost certainly designed to help bear the soul to the land of the dead.

POSITIVE IDENTIFICATION REQUIRED

Balinese are among the peoples who share, in one form or another, the belief that cremation liberates the soul. Because they believe that liberation must precede reincarnation, cremation is a time of joy rather than of mourning.

But unless things are properly arranged before a funeral pyre is lighted, the soul of the deceased may be subjected to great trouble. Elaborate coffins and towers, along with sumptuous feasts for mourners and guests, are required. Persons unable to pay for a suitable cremation may bury their dead for years while saving money for the fiery celebration.

Not only are Balinese cremations extremely expensive, also they require meticulous preparation that often begins years in advance.

An early ritual aimed at eventual cremation involves a special type of priestly dentistry. No later than puberty,

every Balinese tries to go to a temple for "the filing of the teeth." This rite, which involves grinding down the six upper front teeth until they are absolutely even, is considered to be a sure way of identifying a human.

If teeth were not filed, a cremated person might confront the gods with ragged fangs (the marks of a demon) and hence be denied entrance to the spirit world to which fire has conveyed the soul.

YEN + LAND = FIRE

Traditionally dominant in Japan, the Shinto religion places such emphasis upon returning a dead body to Mother Earth from which it came that as recently as a century ago cremation was prohibited by law. Dwindling land resources plus rising cost of funerals has caused a cultural about-face. Emperors who wished to reserve land for the living instead of the dead first encouraged and then tried to require cremation. Instead of a grave, remains of the dead could be put in an urn that required little storage space on the overcrowded island.

For years, Shinto leaders resisted cremation so stoutly that only Buddhist temples and grounds were available as sacred burial places. Christians who died in Japan and were cremated were likely to go into a new and distinctive feature of Japanese churches: the ash vault.

Centuries earlier, Romans turned to cremation in place of burial because they too were running short of good land in desirable places. For a time, urns filled with ashes were solemnly deposited in columbaria, or boxes originally built for pigeons. Retaining the old name, Roman columbaria became increasingly elaborate and artistic. Some were built by funeral clubs, whose members took responsibility for watching over terra-cotta urns arranged in niches.

Regardless of their design and called by whatever name, depositories for urns require vastly less land than cemeteries—where earth burial gobbled up vast tracts of centrally located land in ancient as well as in modern cities.

WATER OF LIFE

Nobel prize winner Rabindranath Tagore offered songs to the river Ganges as "water of life." Considered holy by 350 million Hindus, the fifteen-hundred-mile meandering stream moves more human ashes than any other river on earth.

According to Indian lore, the river came into being when the goddess Ganga descended to earth in order to redeem the souls of some condemned princes and rajahs. Dumped into the mighty stream formed by Ganga, souls of the noblemen were purified, making it possible for them to rise immediately to heaven.

For centuries the banks of the Ganges have harbored innumerable burning ghats. Now often built of concrete or marble slabs that form burning places near the river's edge, these ghats are especially numerous in the holy city of Benares. Practically all are commercially operated.

Bearing a body, a funeral procession that may have come from many miles away reaches a selected ghat. Workmen of low caste cut winding sheets, smear the corpse with clarified butter (or *ghi*), and place it on the pyre. A close relative of the deceased lights a torch, applies it to the head of a dead male's bier, the foot of a dead female's. As the praise of fire is chanted, the body is consumed.

At Benares alone, an average winter day sees ashes of fifty corpses scattered in the sacred Ganges. Water that purifies the souls of the dead is simultaneously used to provide spiritual cleansing for devout pilgrims. For many of them, immersion in holy water that is thick with human ashes is the culmination of a lifelong search for sanctity.

TREE BURIAL

There is no evidence of cultural contact of any sort between natives of Tibet and the Plains Indians of North America. Yet burial practices of the latter had striking points of similarity with those Tibetans who deliberately placed the dead in the air instead of in the ground.

Practiced especially among the Sioux, a warrior who died was placed in a tree and left there for at least a year. Where trees big enough to hold a corpse were scarce, some tribesmen, notably the Chickasaws and the Choctaws, built scaffolds as substitutes for trees.

In sharp contrast with Tibetan customs, "air burials" of American Indians nearly always involved protection of the body against scavengers. A buffalo hide or deer skin was the typical covering for a corpse until trade with the white man brought blankets into use as substitutes.

A warrior "buried" in a tree was usually provided with food and weapons for use in the journey to the afterlife.

About a year after a tree (or scaffold) burial took place, there was a second ceremony. Using suitable incantations, tribesmen removed the semimummified body from its perch and gave it final burial in a cave or a grave.

BURIAL AT SEA

Like air burial, tree burial, and cremation, burial at sea probably got its start as a concession to necessity. Especially in tropical and semitropical regions, a voyage of only a few days was too long to keep a dead man aboard a ship propelled by oars or equipped only with primitive sails.

Once initiated by necessity, burial at sea slowly developed its own set of (largely unwritten) laws and rites. It became almost universally customary for the captain of a ship, no matter what its size, to function in lieu of priest or clergyman. Proper burial at sea began to mean not only a brief service conducted by the captain but also use of waterproof sheets for wrapping a corpse, plus stone or metal with which to send the body promptly to the bottom.

During the great age of sail, in which Europeans explored vast regions of the world by water, standard gear for a long voyage included proper burial items. It was taken for granted that at least one man, and perhaps many would die in faraway waters days or weeks from the nearest land.

Advent of steamers, soon equipped with refrigerated compartments, seemed for a time to spell the end of burial at sea. A crew member, passenger, or fighting man who died aboard ship could be stored until home port was reached.

In recent decades, a new form of sea burial has suddenly become widely popular. Increasing numbers of persons in regions as widely separated as the United States and Australia are stipulating that their bodies be cremated and that their ashes be scattered at sea. Hence the typical sea burial today is from a plane rather than a ship.

AT LEAST THE HEART!

Especially in medieval Europe, survivors who couldn't put a dead man's body six feet under went to great effort to save at least the heart. Special caskets, commonly made of lead but fashioned of precious metal when intended for use of royalty, were shaped as repositories for hearts.

Killed by an arrow from a crossbow while fighting in France in 1199, Richard the Lion-Hearted was many days from home. Following instructions he had prepared in advance, his followers buried his body near the spot where he fell. Embalmed with spices and placed in a casket formed to receive it, his heart went to the city that he loved most—Rouen. Workmen making repairs to Rouen's cathedral in 1838 took the little casket from its niche, opened it long enough to discover that though Richard's great heart had withered like a faded leaf, it had "gained a strange kind of leathery permanence."

The heart of Henry III was buried in Normandy, but Edward I directed that his heart be buried "nowhere on earth except in Jerusalem itself." Robert Bruce wished his heart to be buried in Jerusalem (in the Church of the Holy Sepulcher). On his deathbed he made Sir James Douglas, a trusted lieutenant, vow to carry out that wish. But Douglas was himself killed in battle. The heart of Bruce, enclosed in a silver casket that hung around his neck, was eventually laid to rest not in the Church of the Holy Sepulcher but in Melrose Abbey.

James II of England (1633–1701) magnanimously bequeathed his heart to the convent at Chaillot, which already held as one of its treasured relics the heart of his mother.

RESERVED FOR THE FAITHFUL

Scripture tells us nothing about the background of Deborah, lifelong nurse and companion of Rebekah. Context of the story suggests, however, that she was not an Israelite by either birth or marriage. That may account for the fact that she was buried under an oak tree. For in countless historical situations, holy or even customary burial places have been reserved for members of the faithful, with outsiders or nonbelievers refused space.

Among the children of Israel, even a person born to the faith might, in exceptional cases, be refused burial "in the

BURIAL   43

tombs of his fathers," because of flagrant or conspicuous disobedience of the law of the Lord (see I Kings 13:2–22).

Burial places of medieval Europe, both within walls of cathedrals and in tracts of land adjoining them, were invariably consecrated through formal rites. Throughout Christendom, such holy ground was considered too good for an infidel, a Jew, a murderer, an executioner, or a person who had committed the flagrant sin of taking his own life. Bodies of these persons, plus others who were refused burial by priests in charge of consecrated ground, often went into unmarked graves.

Numerous Christian sects and non-Christian religious groups in possession of cemeteries still try (and frequently do so successfully) to refuse burial to persons not meeting standards of the ruling group.

WITHIN PROTECTIVE WALLS

Because the cathedrals of medieval Europe and Britain were far better protected than open-air cemeteries, great numbers of persons arranged to be interred within the walls of places of worship. Relatives who couldn't arrange to get space for a crypt in a wall often settled for burial beneath the floor of the cathedral. A visit to most of the great cathedrals of the Old World involves, therefore, walking over graves—a practice widely thought to bring bad luck.

Even by utilizing floor space as well as wall space, it was impossible for a major cathedral to take whatever bodies came that way. Increasingly, these highly desirable last resting places within protective walls came to be reserved for persons of wealth and prominence.

England's famous Westminster Abbey is literally jammed and packed with graves of kings, statesmen, military and naval heroes, and other notables of the island kingdom. More

STRANGE FACTS ABOUT DEATH

than three hundred years ago space in Westminster became so scarce that only a ruling monarch could arrange a new burial there.

King Charles I personally promised poet-playwright Ben Jonson that he would be interred in the abbey at a spot of his own choice. Jonson picked what he considered a desirable spot. But at his death on August 6, 1637, it was found that other bodies occupied all the space except "about eighteen inches of square ground." To honor the royal promise, King Charles arranged for Jonson to be buried in a sitting position with his head pointing to the sky.

A FULL COMPLEMENT OF ATTENDANTS

Ur of the Chaldees, the ancient Mesopotamian city that scripture lists as the ancestral home of Abraham, attracted the interest of archaeologists as early as 1854. It wasn't until 1922, however, that an expedition under Leonard Woolley discovered the nearly intact mausoleum of Third Dynasty royalty.

Little disturbed during a period of about forty-five hundred years, the tombs yielded not only bones of kings and queens but also those of numerous attendants and courtiers. Queen Shub-ad and her consort, positively identified, went into the spirit world accompanied by those who had served them in life. Courtiers were dressed in their finest clothing. Musicians took along elaborate harps. Soldiers guarded the royal pair with spears. Even the royal oxcart, pulled by grooms, was placed in the massive burial chamber.

Bones of attendants lay in positions that led Woolley and other scholars to conclude they died peacefully. Perhaps they took sleeping potions and suffocated without awakening or drank poison in order to make sure they could serve Shub-ad in death as in life.

AN INCREDIBLY RARE BOOK

Mayans of pre-Columbian America reached a high level of civilization. Yet they never produced books in quantity. New World materials on which to write were scarce and hard to process. Bark of the fig tree, pounded into a pulp and bonded with gum before being coated with lime, was a rare and costly kind of paper.

Spanish conquerors destroyed all but three of the Mayan books, or codexes, they discovered during centuries of plunder. The three that escaped destruction were sent to Europe.

Near the midpoint of this century, Dr. David Pendergast of Canada's Royal Ontario Museum led a field expedition into the region of Belize, British Honduras. They found several tombs that still held artifacts placed there long ago. One held the body of a man whose gear suggested that he was a high-placed religious leader.

Along with a frog of translucent jade plus beads and ornaments with religious symbols, archaeologists found badly damaged fragments of a Mayan codex. It may be years before fragments are deciphered. Still, the book, believed to have been written about A.D. 700, cherished during life and useful to the soul of its dead owner, is among the rarest of New World literary finds.

MINIATURE MODELS

Ancient Egyptians believed so strongly in a future life that they tried to provide for all needs of their dead. Food and water were often placed in tombs. A dead soldier was likely to be given his favorite weapon, and an expired woman might have her cosmetic jar placed in her hand. Even embalmed pets were put in tombs so that they could continue to give pleasure to their owners in the world beyond.

There's no clear evidence that Egyptians ever followed the Mesopotamian practice of sending large groups of servants and courtiers to their death so that they could accompany kings and queens. But, very early, the people of the Nile decorated tombs with elaborate wall paintings and reliefs that depicted attendants busy at their usual chores.

Later, during the Ninth and Tenth dynasties, it became customary to put trays of miniature models in tombs in lieu of the symbolic paintings and reliefs. Such miniatures showed vassals bringing animals or grain in order to pay their taxes, along with bakers carrying baskets of bread on their heads and servants of both sexes with the paraphernalia of their work. Supposedly, models were provided in order to make sure that persons who had been surrounded by servants during their earthly existence would be equally well treated in the realm of the spirit.

READY FOR A LONG VOYAGE

Tribesmen of northern Europe, heavily dependent upon the sea, gave far more importance to a good ship than to a cart, chariot, or other land vehicle. It was natural, therefore, that men who had spent their lives in command of ships should be buried in them. Ship burials took place in Norway, Sweden, Denmark, Finland, and even England.

During the Viking period a special chamber was likely to be built amidships, in a vessel carefully selected for the longest of all voyages. Laid on a bed, the corpse was surrounded by personal gear such as sword, shield, ax, spear, knife, and whetstone. At Sutton Hoo, England, a ship buried in the seventh century yielded vessels for food and drink plus a gold and enamel purse cover that depicted fantastic creatures of the sea. Vikings practiced cremation as well as burial.

Some ships, prepared according to age-old customs and fully stocked for the journey of the soul, were burned. Ibn Fadlan, an early Arabian traveler to the far North, saw and described the last rites given to a Viking chieftain.

After his ship was beached and put in perfect order, the richly dressed corpse was laid on a carpeted bench. Food and drink of all sorts were placed around the body. A slave woman who had volunteered to accompany her chief to the world beyond was garroted and stabbed. Then torches were put to the ship, and it became a funeral pyre for its master, his slaves, his weapons, his food, and his personal gear.

MENUS VARIED WIDELY

In hundreds of cultures, it has been considered essential to provide food for the spirit of the dead. Types and quantities of foodstuffs used for this purpose have varied so widely that

STRANGE FACTS ABOUT DEATH

nothing even approaching a standard practice for mankind can be identified.

Early rock graves of Canaanites in northern Syria were provided with special windows so that survivors could regularly bring food and drink for the dead. Archaeological evidence indicates that practically all common items of diet were considered suitable for those who had passed from this life into the life beyond.

Classical Greeks were more discriminating. Their only sweetening agent, prized because of its scarcity, was honey. Even a poor man was typically buried with one jar of honey as food for his journey; in the case of rich and powerful persons, graves were likely to be crammed with many jars of the costly stuff.

In rural Mexico, Christians still place gifts of cooked fruit on church altars so that departed loved ones may feast. Toda tribesmen of southern India use buffalo milk as their staple food. So, to them it seems only logical that at least two animals should be slaughtered at the death of a herdsman, giving him a start toward building up a herd of dairy cattle in the spirit world.

SOLDIER'S HORSE

With the mechanization of military forces, a long-established Western custom is vanishing. For centuries, the horse belonging to a deceased officer was solemnly led in his funeral procession.

This practice grew up as a modification of a much older one that involved killing a mount at the time of his warrior's burial. By sacrificing a man's horse, Mongols and Tartars (who were heavily dependent upon horses for their way of life) sought to make sure that the spirit of the animal would go through "the gate of the sky" in order to serve the spirit of its master.

As late as 1871, East European General Kasimer was provided with a mount for use after Kasimer's death. The animal was killed and placed in the grave with the dead general. Followers of Blackbird, a chieftain of the Omaha Indians, went one step further. When the Omahas buried their leader, about 1800, he was interred astride his favorite pony.

OFF TO THE HAPPY HUNTING GROUND— TWENTIETH-CENTURY STYLE

Thomas J. Quinion of Canaan, New York, was proud of his descent from American Indians. So when he died in 1969 at age sixty-four, his son William wanted to send him off to the happy hunting ground in proper style.

Quinion departed from Indian tradition and bowed to the white man's law that requires burial in the earth but insisted on digging the grave himself. Pulled to the graveside by a horse-drawn wagon, the body of the dead man was placed six feet under. With him went his rifle and a supply of ammunition, plus his pipe and a quantity of tobacco. As a final gesture, a supply of matches and his best hat were placed beside the body.

All these things, said the son, would prove useful to the spirit of his father. But twentieth-century influence was clearly evident when a mixing truck pulled alongside the grave and filled it with concrete.

TWENTIETH-CENTURY "CHARIOT BURIAL"

There's no certainty that Sandra Ilene West was acquainted with the ancient custom of chariot burial, but prior to her

STRANGE FACTS ABOUT DEATH

death in 1977 the wealthy eccentric left specific instructions that provided for chariot burial—twentieth-century style.

Her will was specific. Administrators were required by its terms to bury her in San Antonio, adjacent to her late husband. So far, the request was conventional. But in addition to stipulating the place where her remains should be placed, the woman said she wanted to be buried "in my lace nightgown . . . in my Ferarri, with the seat slanted comfortably."

In Los Angeles, where she died, Superior Court Commissioner Franklin E. Dana ruled that her instructions should be followed. "To preserve human dignity," ruled the court, the Ferrari would have to be enclosed in a wooden crate. But inside that crate would be her sports car holding its one-time owner "in the blue lace nightgown that now clothes her remains, in the driver's seat, the seat slanted comfortably to accommodate her remains."

According to the nurse who attended Mrs. West in her final illness, the widow of oil and cattle millionaire Ike West

was an avid student of ancient Egyptian life and was influenced by the fact that pharaohs were typically entombed "with their possessions, their servants, and things to make them comfortable forever."

FORM-FITTING BURIAL BOXES

No one knows when humans first began making containers for bodies of the dead instead of depositing bodies in caves or hewn tombs or other places of safekeeping. Customs according to which burial containers are shaped somewhat like the human body are virtually worldwide, however.

Frequently a person of high rank was given a burial box having body, legs, arms, and head (often highly stylized) with features shaped by a sculptor to resemble the face of the corpse.

Clay and limestone have been widely used for preparation of such coffins. Increasing technological skill led many peoples to turn to precious and semiprecious metals, while others devoted great time and skill to carving form-fitting burial boxes from granite and marble.

Even today in much of Europe the coffin's shape is clearly based upon the shape of the human body—with wide shoulders and a tapering section just wide enough to accommodate the head. Many great cathedrals hold remains of rulers and saints in elaborately carved marble coffins that are complete with busts of the occupants.

Development of the rectangular coffin, whose physical appearance in no way resembles that of a human's body, is recent and Western in origin.

STURDIEST OF NATURAL MATERIALS

Stone is the sturdiest of natural materials. Because of its time-defying qualities, stone was used to mark graves at least as early as the dawn of prehistorical times. (A casual reading of the Old Testament reveals that stones were commonly used for landmarks and to commemorate notable events. Along with stones used to mark places of burial, many were put to use in the shape formed by nature.)

Development of metal tools, notably of iron, fostered a major change. Instead of stones from the field, shaped stones with inscribed messages came into use. These primitive forerunners of the modern machine-made tombstone were in wide use long before the time of Christ.

During a period of a few centuries, no notable or prosperous European or American was buried without an elaborate tombstone with many lines of praise or biographical data. In the case of persons buried within cathedral walls, the marble coffin lid often doubled as tombstone and might have its entire surface covered with "time-defying" tributes.

Escalating costs of polished and inscribed tombstones, which require a great deal of costly labor, have caused survivors to erect smaller, less ornate, and less verbose grave markers. Ostensibly for the sake of "permanent" natural beauty but actually in order to foster cost-cutting, many memorial parks now bar old-fashioned tombstones entirely.

ALL SIZES, SHAPES, AND COLORS

Coffins in which the dead are laid before or during funeral rites come not only in all kinds of shapes; they vary widely in size and even in color. Tribesmen of Ecuador paint the coffin of a child white but use magenta or orange for the coffin of an adult.

Until the coming of Communism to China, a person getting along in years typically selected his coffin long before death. For centuries the best ones were made from four half logs carefully fitted together. Since wood might be three to five inches thick, a really good coffin was likely to weigh three hundred pounds or more.

The closing of the coffin lid was a particularly crucial activity in ancient China. Bystanders typically took several steps backward or even went into another room. Their caution grew out of firm belief that a person's health would be endangered if his shadow should be enclosed in a coffin along with a corpse.

Plain wooden boxes (usually narrow at the head and feet and wide at the shoulders) were in general use for many centuries. Amish of strict beliefs still employ such a box—hand-made after the corpse has been measured with a stick or with two pieces of string.

Elaborately carved wooden coffins of Victorian England varied in price according to the material from which they were made: oak, elm, agba, chestnut, or some less common and more costly wood. Mahogany coffins have come into wide use only in modern times. Heavy-gauged metal ones (preferably copper or bronze), often lowered into "waterproof" cement vaults, are modern and American in origin. Whether these rectangular metal boxes will preserve bodies longer than ancient Egyptian mummy cases, only the passing centuries will tell.

URNS AND JARS

As practiced in a great many diverse cultural settings, preparation for a funeral has involved finding (and using) a suitable urn or jar rather than a coffin.

In Bible lands, special jars of pottery large enough to contain the body of an adult (whose bones had been removed) were manufactured in immense numbers. Huge jars found at the site of ancient Gebal (present-day Byblos) held bodies typically given a posture that Freudian psychologists tend to compare with the fetal state.

Bodies of children and infants were placed in smaller jars. At Tepe Gawra, archaeologists have found one tiny skeleton curled up in what was probably an ordinary bowl for use in the household.

Concurrently with the use of such jars, both large and small, other peoples of the early Iron Age began to put the ashes of their cremated dead into food pots. Gradually the shape of these pots was changed so that distinctive burial urns were produced.

During the long and bloody U.S. involvement in Southeast Asia, many battlefield dispatches came from or referred to the Plain of Jars in Laos. By the time it became a focal point of mechanized warfare, few newspaper correspondents bothered to point out that the name was conferred because so many huge ceremonial burial jars were placed in this area during a period of many centuries.

FEET FIRST

Even though the spirit of a dead man may have to be ferried over water, and regardless of whether his body is buried or burned, he will sooner or later have to walk toward an eternal destination. In a great many cultures having few other elements in common, it has been customary (sometimes mandatory) for pallbearers to move a corpse feet first.

To move a dead person head first, according to widespread beliefs, would hamper the spirit's journey on foot. Elaborately codified in medieval Christendom, this ancient and essentially pagan concept was interpreted to mean that anything other than a feet-first movement of a corpse would actually endanger the soul of the deceased.

In many times and places, it has been considered essential

that the funeral procession move in the same direction as the path of the sun. Burial with the head facing east—still widely practiced in the modern West—leaves feet of the corpse facing toward the point where the sun sets, in symbolic readiness to walk that way.

Monuments

FORTY-FIVE-HUNDRED-YEAR-OLD ENIGMA

Man's most immense single monument, the Great Pyramid of Egypt, is generally credited to Cheops, a pharaoh of the Fourth Dynasty. Since earlier and smaller pyramids functioned exclusively as tombs, the Great Pyramid is widely believed to have been designed to hold and to guard the remains of Cheops.

His cartouche, roughly equivalent to a signature in stone,

supports the theory by its presence. So does an immense stone coffin, big enough to hold a mummy case.

Sprawling over more than thirteen acres and rising to forty stories in height, the pyramid was built from 2.5 million stone blocks. Ranging in weight from 4,000 to 140,000 pounds, each block is individually fitted with great precision. Facing stones (enough to cover twenty-two acres) were stripped off long ago and used to build most of the major buildings of old Cairo. Gross weight of the pyramid is about 6.75 million tons, yet after more than forty-five hundred years its base is level within one-half inch.

Herodotus, the famous Greek historian, said that 100,000 men built the Great Pyramid during a period of twenty years. To do that, workmen would have had to place about 1,000 tons of stone per day with never a holiday.

Though it has been the subject of hundreds of books, no one knows positively how Cheops raised the world's biggest monument—or what functions it served in addition to perpetuating a name that otherwise would long ago have been forgotten.

MORE SPLENDID IN DEATH THAN IN LIFE

As kings go, Tutankhamen was insignificant. He was so young when he succeeded to the throne of Egypt, about 1358 B.C., that a regent made most decisions. Ay, the regent, gained the throne upon the death of his youthful master.

Probably through the agency of Ay, the short-lived monarch was placed in a mortuary temple in the Valley of the Kings, near Luxor. Near the entrance to his tomb, a portrait head of Tutankhamen depicted him as springing from a lotus flower. An exquisite calcite bowl bearing his Egyptain names include hieroglyphic characters that wished, "May thy ka (soul) live and mayest thou spend millions of years, thou lover of Thebes, sitting with thy face to the north wind and thine eyes envisioning felicity."

Virtually untouched for nearly thirty-three hundred years, Tutankhamen's tomb was discovered in 1922 by George E. S. M. Herbert and Howard Carter. Inside they found a sarcophagus of three magnificent coffins set one within another—the innermost one being of solid gold. Human-shaped, it bore a painted likeness of its occupant. Fabulous treasures were packed inside the tomb: golden chariots, beds, flowers, and a jewel-encrusted golden throne.

Legend to the contrary, Europeans who ransacked the lost burial place were not felled one by one by effects of a mysterious curse of the pharaoh. Instead, their discovery fostered the goal of those who buried their king in such luxury so long ago. Fame of the archaeological find has made the name of otherwise obscure King Tut better known than that of many more powerful monarchs of more recent times.

QUALITY RATHER THAN QUANTITY

Mausolus, a relatively obscure ruler of a region of Asia Minor, made no great impact upon life in the fourth century B.C. But his death triggered actions destined to have a lasting effect. His sister and widow, Artemisia, engaged the world's finest artists, sculptors, builders, and workers in bronze.

They were told to design and build the most exquisite tomb man had ever seen. Size was not an objective. Artemisia wanted quality, not quantity. Her emphasis led to a marble tomb so rich with color and suggested movement that persons who saw it for the first time exclaimed over it as an abode of life, not death.

Above a flat-topped marble pyramid stood a four-horse chariot with Mausolus himself holding the reins. Sculptured friezes surged with movement: an attacking warrior with calf muscles bulging, a chariot race complete with straining horses and eager riders, Amazons hacking at their foes, and Centaurs in full combat. Many of these vivid pieces of sculpture were alive with color: red, gold, and green.

Though diminutive by comparison with the Great Pyramid, the monument planned by Artemisia joined that of Cheops as one of the Seven Wonders of the Ancient World. Christians plundered the tomb in the fifteenth century, later razed it in order to burn marble blocks for production of lime. By then the name of otherwise obscure Mausolus had become so famous that every mausoleum, elaborate or simple, perpetuates it.

A MONUMENTAL STRIKEOUT

No one knows precisely when or why Egyptians invented the mythological creature they called the sphinx. That mystery, plus the enigmatic and stylized look linked with the creature, accounts for English-language use of the word to label a person who is beyond comprehension by others.

A typical Egyptian sphinx was a compound creature with the body of a lion and the head of a man. Greeks who adopted the sphinx often gave it wings and a female head and bust.

Probably the earliest representations of the lion-man were intended to symbolize the god Horus, one of whose roles was to stand watch over temples and tombs. Some long-lost ruler had a brilliant idea: in order both to honor Horus and to immortalize himself, he would create a sphinx bearing his own features. Dozens, perhaps hundreds, of such monuments were erected. As rulers go, King Senusret III (1879–1841 B.C.) was of minor importance. He scored a triumph, though, because the sphinx that portrays him can still be clearly identified.

Near the Great Pyramid at Giza stand the remains of the most enormous sphinx ever created. Both the body and head are carved from solid rock—especially resistant to deterioration. This gigantic monument measures about 240 feet in length, stands 66 feet high. The face alone is nearly 14 feet wide.

Like nearly every other Egyptian sphinx, this one clearly portrayed a ruler. Size of the monument indicates that he was (for his era) a very great and powerful pharaoh. But as a device to perpetuate his memory, the Great Sphinx represents a strikeout. Though mentioned in literature since 2900 B.C., the monument bears the face of a pharaoh whose name has never been discovered.

SECONDHAND STATUES

In every epoch and in all parts of the world, statues have been valued as especially vivid and lasting monuments. Truly enduring ones are made of stone or of metal, but in regions where stone is rare or technology for its work has not developed, statues of wood are common. Many notable ones have been commissioned and purchased by persons they represent. Others have been erected by admiring followers.

Usually—but not always—a statue is a reasonably accurate representation of the person whose memory it perpetuates.

During the era when Mussolini was rising to power in Italy, a soccer team from Innsbruck, Austria, scored a stunning triumph over an Italian team from Milan. Italians responded by sending the victors a huge cast-iron statue of Il Duce. There was just one difficulty: the people of Innsbruck positively refused to have Mussolini's statue erected in their

city. So a cast-iron beard was cast for the statue and it found a prominent place in a park as a memorial to Gambrinus, locally credited with having been the inventor of beer.

In Ecuador, admirers of the poet Olmeda wanted to honor him with a statue but couldn't raise enough money to get the work done. Since one of Olmeda's followers lived in London, he was commissioned to search the city for a secondhand statue. It took only a few weeks to find a nearly new one that depicts Lord Byron. Purchased and shipped across the Atlantic, it was erected in Guayaquil, Ecuador, and altered only by having the name *Olmeda* engraved on its base.

A ZEALOUS CONVERT

Constantine the Great became one of six claimants to the throne of Rome in A.D. 306. Six years later he was converted to Christianity. Long-standing tradition says he saw in the sky a cross with the message "In hoc signo vinces" ("By this sign thou shalt conquer").

Conquer he did. Defeating external and internal foes one after another, he was sole emperor of the West before the end of the year in which he saw the vision. A decade later he was master of the entire Roman world.

As emperor, Constantine called the famous Council of Nicaea, A.D. 325, in which the Nicene Creed, or statement of Christian faith, was adopted. Then in gratitude for victories won by the God he now worshiped, he set out to find and mark the exact location of Jesus' burial place. His spiritual advisor, Bishop Macarius, decided that the simple tomb owned by Joseph of Arimathea, in which Jesus' body lay just three days, once lay under a huge temple to Aphrodite that was built in the second century.

Constantine had the pagan temple razed. Since Calvary and the tomb of Jesus were only about sixty feet apart, he erected on the site two splendid churches. Completed about 336, they were intended to stand forever.

But Persians damaged both structures when they captured Jerusalem in 614. During a later period of Moslem occupation, Constantine's memorials to Jesus were practically destroyed. Crusaders made repairs and enlargements in the eleventh century, only to see Saladin the Great add them to the Moslem empire in 1187. Today they are held by Israel. Perhaps the world's most fought-over shrine, the Church of the Holy Sepulcher still marks the spot a one-time pagan judged to have held the briefly used tomb of Jesus.

ROYAL FREE-LOADER

Ever since Westerners discovered the Taj Mahal at Agra, India, and dubbed it the most beautiful building in the world, lovers have told and retold the story of the two who lived together and who now will lie together for eternity.

Shah Jahan, fifth emperor of Hindustan in the Mogul dynasty, had many wives. His love was reserved, however, for one: Mumtaz Mahall ("the ornament," or "the distinguished one"). At her death in 1631, Shah Jahan vowed to place her body in the loveliest structure ever seen. It was white, the color of mourning, and represented the work of the finest architects and craftsmen, not only of China, Persia, and Turkey but also of France and Italy.

Deposed by his son Aurangzeb in 1658, the builder of the Taj Mahal and one-time occupant of the Peacock Throne was imprisoned until his death two years later. Abundant evidence indicates that he intended to build for himself a separate tomb—black, to symbolize his conquests that had brought Mogul power to its highest point.

As successor to the throne, Aurangzeb had no intention of wasting a fortune in order to commemorate his father. At his order, Shah Jahan was placed beside his favorite wife—not as the final act in a beautiful love story, but because their son felt a tomb built for one could serve as well for two.

"BROKEN FACTORY CHIMNEY" FINALLY FINISHED

By unanimous vote of the Continental Congress in 1783, U.S. leaders agreed that George Washington should be commemorated by a suitable monument. Most lawmakers favored placing an equestrian statue in a conspicuous part of the permanent Capitol. But at Washington's death in 1799 it was estimated that such a monument would cost every American twenty-five cents. That estimate was so high that nothing was done.

John Marshall headed a group of concerned citizens who revived the idea in 1833, forming the Washington National

STRANGE FACTS ABOUT DEATH

Monument Society. During three years, public subscriptions yielded $28,000. That was enough to spark competition for a design. Robert Mills won with a plan for an elaborate statuary-dotted pedestal topped by a six-hundred-foot obelisk.

Plans for statuary were scrapped and the society concentrated on an obelisk. Enough money was raised for construction to begin in 1847. That year, President Polk presided at the laying of a 24,500-pound marble cornerstone.

Six years later the obelisk rose 152 feet into the sky. But in the four succeeding years those who wanted a world-famous memorial to the Father of His Country contributed just $285—and added only 4 feet to the monument, using marble of an inferior grade. It was during this era that Mark Twain described the edifice as being "like a factory chimney with the top broken off." It remained that way for twenty-one years.

Centennial enthusiasm spurred Congress to make a

belated appropriation. Even with forty-five feet subtracted from original plans, when the monument was finished 105 years after the first vote to commemorate Washington, the obelisk that bears his name became the world's tallest structure.

UNFIT FOR A LEADER OF FREE MEN

Andrew Jackson probably heard rumors about the plans of Commodore Jesse D. Elliott before he left the White House in March, 1837. Elliott, a career naval officer, wanted to do something to show his admiration of Jackson. When in Beirut, Lebanon, he came across what he considered a strikingly beautiful third-century tomb carved from two pieces of Greek marble. Decorated with looped garlands, clusters of fruit, and plump cherublike figures, it was said to have been prepared as the burial place of the Roman Emperor Severus.

Elliott bought the big tomb in 1837 and a year later brought it across the sea aboard the U.S.S. *Constitution*. In Washington he relinquished the treasure to custody of the Patent Office, stipulating that it be used as the final resting place of Jackson.

Old Hickory had hinted that he wanted nothing to do with the imported tomb, but it was not until a few months before his death in 1845 that he formally quashed the dream of Commodore Elliott. Writing to his admirer he said, "I cannot consent that my mortal body shall be laid in a repository prepared for an Emperor or King—my republican feelings and principles forbid it."

Jackson instructed that he be buried simply at his beautiful Nashville estate, the Hermitage. His rejected tomb was placed on grounds of the Smithsonian Institution with a plaque noting that he had refused to occupy it.

WORLD'S MOST VISITED TOMB

Nikolai Lenin was a key figure in the famous October Revolution that led to the overthrow of the czarist regime in Russia. It was Lenin (son of a schoolteacher) who came up with the idea of establishing councils, or *soviets*, in the numerous independent republics formed from old Russia.

At his death in 1924, the man now revered as father of the Soviet Union was already widely honored. His followers had his body embalmed by special methods and made plans for a great memorial tomb that they hoped to erect in Moscow. When completed, the tomb was dwarfed by the towering spires of old cathedrals and by the walls of the Kremlin. But Lenin's body, sealed in heavy glass, had a magnetic attraction that even the most ardent Soviet leaders had not fully anticipated.

On a typical day, visitors come to Moscow from other cities of the Soviet Union, lining up at 5:00 A.M. for the privilege of getting a glimpse of Lenin's face. To the Soviet citizen, a visit to Lenin's tomb is like a pilgrimage to the Vatican for a Catholic or a pilgrimage to Mecca for a Moslem.

All day long, every day of the year, men, women, and children shuffle reverently into the tomb that is guarded around the clock by soldiers. In a land that is overtly atheistic, Nikolai Lenin has been regarded with the veneration typically linked only with great religious leaders. His tomb, which attracts more visitors than any other in the world, has been transformed by Soviets into a strangely paradoxical version of a religious shrine that is the "holy ground" of atheistic communism.

OLDEST CHRISTIAN MEMENTO OF DEATH

St. Helena, mother of the Roman emperor Constantine, helped to set in motion the still-thriving wave of popular piety that comes to focus in the Holy Land. Places and events linked with the life of Jesus, usually identified only by tradition, became focal points for visits of pilgrims. The Church of the Holy Sepulcher, said to have been erected to mark the spot where Jesus' body lay briefly in the grave, was a monument to the perseverance of Helena as well as to her faith in the resurrected Lord.

Generations of keepers of the Church of the Holy Sepulcher found new and great marvels from the past. Of those linked with death, not even the traditional tomb of Lazarus challenges the antiquity of another holy spot long pointed out to pilgrims by guides. For a chamber of this hallowed church was identified as the depository of Adam's tomb.

In his famous and often ironic *Innocents Abroad,* Mark Twain addressed himself to the significance of this oldest Christian memento of death:

The tomb of Adam! how touching it was, here in a land of strangers, far away from home and friends! True, he was a blood relation; though a distant one, still a relation! The fountain of my filial affection was stirred to its profoundest depths, and I gave way to tumultuous emotion. I deem it no shame to have wept over the grave of my poor dead relative. Noble old man—he did not live to see his child; and I—I—I, alas! did not live to see him. Let us trust he is better off where he is.

Adam's tomb, subject of these musings, was long ago stricken from "official" lists of certified shrines but is still pointed out by many who make their living as professional guides.

Cities of the Dead

ROCK TOMBS GOOD FOREVER

Nearly a century ago, early archaeologists found rock tombs of the valley of Hinnom in the Holy Land almost impossible to comprehend. According to the best guess of scholars, at least part of the immense necropolis there dates from the era when Jebusites held control of the region.

Unlike a grave dug into the earth or even a shelf within a natural cave, a well-cut rock tomb (actually hollowed out of solid rock) seemed to be good forever to the lucky people who had it.

Actually, in many cases such tombs far outlasted their tenants. When Israelites swept over and conquered the valley of Hinnom, they soon began to remove Jebusite bones from graves. Bodies of Israelites were deposited in the nearly new tombs; some of them probably remained there for many centuries.

During the Crusades, there were periods when these same tombs were in Christian hands. Many warriors died in battle, and numerous pilgrims later died of exhaustion plus disease. What more natural than to remove bones of long-dead Israelites in order to make room for good Christian folk?

Used, emptied, and reused in cycles that followed periods of invasion and war, some ancient rock tombs of Palestine probably had dozens or even scores of occupants. By the twentieth century, most bones were gone. During the 1890s a French writer noted that in these places, "though the dead have long disappeared, their abodes are still entire."

A MAN-MADE LITTLE MOUNTAIN

Marathon, a plain on the northeast coast of ancient Attica, was separated from the plain of Athens by a mountain range. Its name is perpetuated by the international Marathon games.

King Darius of Persia sent a mighty army to punish the Athenians for insubordination late in the fifth century B.C. Athenians called out their full levy of nine thousand heavy infantry and asked neighboring city-states to send help. Response was so poor that a force numbering little more than ten thousand men met fifty thousand heavily armed Persian troops on the plain of Marathon in 490 B.C.

Totally unexpected victory by Athenian forces triggered the famous twenty-eight-mile run that brought news of Persian defeat to the city that was then the cultural center of the Western world. Persians suffered at least 6,400 casualties against 192 deaths in ranks of the Athenians. No one knows what happened to bodies of the slain Persians. But mortal remains of the 192 Athenians were reverently piled together, and then covered with earth and stones. Centuries passed. New waves of invaders swept back and forth across the region that included the little man-made mountain, or *soros*. Persons living in the region forgot how it had been created.

Archaeologists who excavated the burial mound in 1891–1892 found that Athenians killed at Marathon more than two thousand years earlier had been given places in a "village" of the dead with few if any parallels in Europe.

Evidence indicates that all 192 of the heroes who fell before the Persians, were interred at the one spot, which originally was complete with a 30' X 3' trench for funeral offerings.

HIGHWAYS LINED WITH TOMBS

Situated on seven hills on both sides of the Tiber River about sixteen miles from its mouth, Rome was a city of some size at least as early as the eighth century B.C. Ruled as an Etruscan city-state and as a republic before becoming the capital of the Roman Empire, the city proper was surrounded by the Servian wall.

From very early times, unwritten law (gradually committed to writing and codified before being condensed to form "The Twelve Tables") included a stipulation uncommon among the ancients. No burial, not even ashes of a cremated person, might take place within the Servian wall.

Cemeteries, at first small, sprang up at distances of two or three miles from the heart of the city. By the time Caesar's legions first attempted to invade faraway Britain, in 55 B.C., commercial and political activity was causing the population of the capital to soar. Growing numbers of inhabitants meant increasing deaths.

Obedient to ancient prohibitions concerning burial within the city's wall, Romans multiplied the size of early cemeteries and laid out new ones. Like old ones, new cemeteries were commonly located close to highways. As a result, by early centuries of the Christian era a traveler who came to Rome for the first time was likely to be astonished at having to pass through a city of the dead in order to reach the vibrant, throbbing city of the living. Not simply the Via Appia, but all main highways leading into Rome were lined with tombs crowded helter-skelter against one another as burial space grew increasingly scarce.

HOUSES AND SHOPS LONG GONE

Known to modern Westerners as Thebes (actually a Greek title bestowed on it comparatively late), the ancient Egyptian metropolis of No-Amen consisted of two distinct cities. On the east bank of the river was situated the city of the living—houses, shops, taverns, brothels, and warehouses almost invariably constructed from sun-dried brick.

Houses and shops went the way of all flesh many centuries ago. Bricks from which they were made disintegrated, often leaving no trace even of the foundation of a large building.

Quite a different mode of building was employed on the west bank of the river. There, many pharaohs and a great host of lesser notables were placed at death. Houses erected to shelter their spirits were made of cut stone. Designed to last, many of them remained in surprisingly good condition for generations after sun-dried brick homes of artisans who built the tombs had mingled with the sand of the desert.

Many of the sumptuous tombs erected in the city of the dead attached to ancient No-Amen were marvels of architecture and of sculpture. Most faced the river, with their backs to the nearly vertical sandstone cliffs behind. Hatshepsut's tomb had successive tiers of columns. Huge statues flanked the spirit abode of Amenhotep III. Like the tombs themselves, these decorative features so successfully defied time that when Europeans first stumbled upon the great royal cemetery they wondered why it should have been built at a spot so far from an urban center.

UNDERGROUND: IN LIFE AS WELL AS DEATH

Because the world's most famous catacombs are located in Rome, it is widely assumed that these structures designed for multiple burial originated when early Christians had to "go underground." Actually, catacombs had been built and widely used many centuries earlier (notably, among the Etruscans). Decisive proof is lacking, but weight of evidence points to the likelihood that persecuted Christians took to underground worship because they had ready-made havens that were earlier constructed to shelter their dead.

A typical catacomb consisted of a big and sprawling network of corridors interspersed with chambers. Many (but not all) corridors were about three feet wide—but might be as much as forty or fifty feet high.

Horizontal recessess, or compartments, were cut into catacomb walls, often several tiers high. Their size was standardized very early; these compartments (or loculi) were designed to accommodate four corpses. Loculi were equipped with panels, and these panels made ideal places on which to place Christian symbols: the fish, the shepherd, the monogram of Christ.

Chapels carved out underground for use of families and congregations, perhaps in some instances before it became dangerous to be identified as a Christian, served as ideal places for the celebration of the Eucharist and for group worship in times of persecution. Partly because they very early began placing their dead deep underground in accessible catacombs, living Christians had ready-made places of refuge when wisdom dictated that they go underground.

REVEALED BY A HORSE

Not in Rome only but in major cities throughout the empire of which it was the center, early Christians dug catacombs that served as burial places plus havens for refuge and for forbidden worship.

At the little-known city of Sousse in Tunisia, the horse belonging to a colonel of the Fourth Tirailleurs (a unit of the

French army of occupation) fell into a hole during the heyday of the French Foreign Legion. Efforts to rescue the valuable animal revealed that he had stumbled into the single exit by which Christians entered catacombs of the city for a period of about 150 years, beginning shortly before or after A.D. 50.

Totally unknown to moderns until its presence was revealed by the horse, the maze of burial places underneath the site of what was once called Hadrumetum stretches for more than a mile. Like the catacombs of Rome, tunnels hewn from rock are lined with burial niches and are interspersed with chambers that long served as chapels.

Wealthy Christians of this Roman-African community were buried in decent levels of three, one above the other. These resting places were given plaques bearing the names of occupants: Sorica, Victorina, Heraclius, Gudulus, Renata, and the like. Relatives who couldn't afford plaques arranged for their dead to be given mass burial in unmarked chambers

STRANGE FACTS ABOUT DEATH

and pits into some of which hundreds of bodies were placed.

Time erased most differences between rich and poor; bones of all turned into a sort of porous red clay that crumbles between the fingers. Tangible evidence of the number of occupants of this underground city of the dead consists chiefly of innumerable outlines of bodies, clearly and indelibly impressed upon surfaces of rock ledges.

FOURTEEN-HUNDRED-FOOT GREAT SERPENT

Early tribes of North America, typically but not universally nomadic, had vast areas in which to go about the activities of the living and to store the bodies of the dead. Unlike Old World cities like Rome and Cairo, there was no shortage of land that could be used for burial. Yet in many regions it became cutomary to deposit great numbers of bodies in selected sites, rather than to dig solitary graves or to follow the custom of tree burial.

Along the western and southern rims of the Great Lakes, spreading southward between the Appalachians and the Mississippi River, at least 100,000 burial mounds were erected at vast labor. Some of them, like stone monuments of Egypt, served as final resting places for powerful chieftains.

Others took the characteristic shape of the man-made mound during a period of centuries in which corpse after corpse was deposited at a designated spot, typically covered with earth in each case. Early explorers didn't recognize these mounds as being man-made; new ones, often very large, are constantly being discovered.

Especially for the burial of a chief, a mound might be given the shape of a totemic animal (reptile, bird, animal, or fish). One of the most famous of these is the great serpent mound in southern Ohio, which coils for fourteen hundred feet. Once built for a person of importance, a mound was likely to become a burial place for ordinary tribesmen. Though some seem to have been built for the same purpose, Indian mounds of North America differ from pyramids of Egypt in that most of the former came to include large numbers of dead for whom no lasting clues to identification were provided.

"BELONGING TO THE LORD HIMSELF"

In the aftermath of the Protestant Reformation, followers of Martin Luther and other bitter opponents of the Roman Church established their own cemeteries or took possession of existing ones and expanded them. By the time an English traveler wrote one of the earliest (1617) personal descriptions of rural Germany, he reported that "they have attached to many a City a beautiful place to bury their dead, called Gods-aker, vulgarly spelled Gotts-aker."

That title stems from German *Gottesacker,* a title long applied to any "seed-field of the Lord" in which bodies of the faithful are "sown" to wait for the general resurrection (see I Cor. 15:36–44).

Especially in Britain and her early colonies, many cemeteries were laid out so that they would be 4,840 square yards, one acre, in size. This made it easy and natural to use the German-born title to designate a place of mass burial. As population rose and cities expanded in size, old boundary lines of cemeteries were moved time and again.

Many a burial place expanded to several acres in size, and then to scores of acres. Vividness of the hoary title indicating divine "ownership" of a cemetery, no matter what its size, has caused it to linger in popular speech. Annually, Moravians whose ancestors (biological and spiritual) are buried in what is now Winston-Salem, North Carolina, gather at Easter for "the grooming of God's acres." Incised

STRANGE FACTS ABOUT DEATH

lettering of headstones that have spilled far past the limits of a single acre are scoured with toothbrushes in preparation for a sunrise service in the cemetery that attracts thousands of worshipers—so many that musicians alone may number five hundred or more.

FOCAL POINT OF LONG-GONE COMMUNITY

Westward expansion of the U.S. frontier, notably during the century following the American Revolution, led to establishment of thousands of rural communities. Each had at least one cemetery, typically located adjacent to a church house.

Population trends that have in the last few generations led to abandonment of the countryside in favor of the city have wiped out many once-thriving settlements and churches. Almost always, the cemetery far outlives the community that produced it.

Most of these rural burial places are attached to Protestant churches, many of which have long been abandoned as places of worship. But through cemetery associations, survivors and relatives frequently keep burial places tended, occasionally adding a new grave when a native of the community dies in a town or city and leaves instructions that he or she be interred in a village of the dead that perpetuates the memory of what was once a village of the living.

BLOOD KIN ONLY

Great numbers of burial places not affected by religious or economic barriers are not open to the general public. Generally owned outright (instead of rented), with title passing from generation to generation, the typical family burial place is restricted to blood kin.

One of the important acts of Abraham was the purchase of the Cave of Machpelah for use as a family sepulcher. Abraham first used it for the body of Sarah; then he himself was buried in it, with Isaac, Rebekah, Jacob, and Leah following. Scriptural accounts make it clear that the burial place was personal property; there is no indication that servants of foreigners were buried there as long as it remained in the hands of Abraham's descendants.

Municipal cemeteries of large European cities often sold designated space to families. In the case of Paris, very early troubled by shortage of burial space, typical family vaults were built to hold twenty caskets. Inevitably, these became overcrowded as generations passed. So statutes were enacted permitting that ten years after a vault was filled, bones from its twenty caskets could be placed into one, making room for nineteen new burials of blood relatives.

Wide-open spaces of the American frontier produced the family plot. Most prevalent in the United States, but not limited to it, such a burial place was usually created along with a farm and might be located close to the farmhouse. A special headache for builders of interstate highways, remains of bodies interred in such family plots have often had to be dug up and moved to make way for semitrailers and private cars.

NO ACCESS BY LAND

San Michele Cemetery (municipally owned and operated) in Venice may be the world's only major burial place that can't be reached by a conventional hearse. San Michele is an island of the dead.

A gondola or a barge-shaped craft usually serves as

"floating hearse." Like the cemetery, special funeral craft are owned and operated by the city.

Unlike cities that insist upon absolute control, Venice has permitted the formation of a private burial organization with a truly formidable name: Arciconfraternita di S. Cristofore Compagnia della Misericordia. Members pay nominal dues and are permitted to transport the dead in a black-draped motorboat belonging to the society.

Accessible only by water, San Michele almost seems to represent in modern form the ancient voyages in which Charon the boatman (who never worked gratis) was alone responsible for transporting souls of the dead to the great beyond.

UPWARD RATHER THAN OUTWARD

Rozzano, Italy, an incorporated town within the area of metropolitan Milan, was running short of grave space even while it remained a small town. By 1969, city fathers grappling with a 400 percent increase in population during fifteen years, faced the inevitable: some day, most of these newcomers would need to be buried.

Like many Old World centers (and increasing numbers of cities in the New World), Rozzanno faced a critical shortage of land. So a series of municipal elections led to a decision that their cemetery would expand upward rather than outward.

Architects drew up plans for a five-story circular tower much like some of the world's most modern hotels. They provided room for precisely 3,120 residents—all to be permanent. Probably the world's first high-rise cemetery, the Rozzano idea has since spread widely. Increasingly, city planners are looking to the sky rather than to the ground as they try to take into account the never-ceasing need for places in which to provide for long-term storage of the dead.

LAND RECLAIMED BY RED CHINESE

Reverence and superstition combined have typically operated to block defilement or pillage of graves (except by professional grave robbers).

Land reform was a major promise made by Chinese Communists who overthrew the nationalist government. Even in 1949, when the Chinese People's Republic was established, Western news agencies had difficulty getting detailed and authentic information. Enough trickled out, however, to indicate that Red Chinese succeeded in reclaiming substantial tracts of land in and near major cities.

They did it by sending heavy earth-moving equipment to cemeteries, some of which stretched for dozens of acres. Tombstones and other markers were removed, and an attempt was made to remove human bones from the ground. Officially reported to have been buried in a common grave, many such bones were unofficially said to have been ground into fertilizer.

Transformed into fertile farm land, big tracts that once served as cities of the dead help to produce food for China's still growing population.

SIX FOR THE MONEY

California lawmakers years ago enacted statutes that stipulated that a minimum of six bodies is required to constitute a legal cemetery. Small families often buried one or two or three members on isolated farms, but any person wishing to operate a commercial burial place had to begin with a minimum of half a dozen customers.

Missouri-born Hubert Eaton, son of a Baptist minister, had dreams of expansion even before he took over an ailing commercial cemetery in Glendale, California. He soon pushed Forest Lawn past three hundred acres in size, then began to look about for places in which to open branches. In Covina, California, news of his plan to take his highly advertised funeral program to that city leaked out before he could get a cemetery permit. While pickets paraded in protest, his men managed to bury six bodies on property he had already acquired. Since that legally transformed the place into a cemetery, additional protests were useless.

Eaton himself was buried at the home office, the original Forest Lawn, in 1966 after his death (as a multimillionaire) at age eighty-five. Widely known as "the original upbeat undertaker" whose frequently expressed motive was that of "erasing all signs of mourning," the man whose Covina branch was launched by knowledge of the law was also a master of persuasion. Running counter to centuries-old traditions, he advertised chapels of Forest Lawn as especially suitable for weddings—and lived to see more than fifty thousand couples united in the seven buildings originally erected for funeral services.

ROUND-THE-CLOCK DIGGING

Before the progress of modern medicine made deadly epidemics rare, an urban center hard hit by any communicable disease found disposal of the dead a problem which mounted until the peak of the epidemic was reached.

Daniel Defoe, best remembered for his famous *Robinson Crusoe,* liked to think of himself as a forerunner of today's investigative reporter. In that spirit he wrote in 1721 *The Journal of the Plague Year,* filled with vivid details of personal experiences during the great plague that swept over London half a century earlier.

According to Defoe, parish carts creaked through the cobblestone streets late at night. Hoarse-voiced gravediggers shouted monotonously, "Bring out your dead!" When a cart was filled, said the great writer, bodies were dumped, typically by moonlight, into great pits dug for the purpose in unconsecrated ground.

Since in some plague years some cities lost one third of their inhabitants, there is little doubt that contagious diseases led to the first well-documented instances of mass burial (without coffins and minus grave markers) in modern Christian Europe.

A mass grave produced as a side effect of the ravages of typhus or some other plague was usually regarded as community property, but such a "city of nameless and faceless citizens" didn't get the same care as that given to parish cemeteries.

WORLD'S BIGGEST MASS GRAVE

Russian soldiers plus inhabitants of present-day Stalingrad faced insuperable odds when Germans attacked the city during World War II. In spite of initial stubborn resistance, Hitler was so sure of ultimate victory that he selected the building in which he and his generals would celebrate that victory and even drew up plans for table assignments.

Hitler and his officers never ate that feast. During one of the most fearful periods of modern times, "The Thousand Days," persons in the besieged city literally gave everything they had in its defense. Food became so scarce that the daily ration for an adult civilian was reduced to one half of one slice of bread. Though no statistics were kept, it is likely that more persons died of starvation and disease than from German bullets.

A large pit dug for disposal of unmarked bodies was soon filled; so gangs of workers constantly expanded it—only to see new space crowded with fresh bodies of men, women, and children. Before the fearful carnage was halted by German withdrawal, Stalingrad had become the site of the world's biggest mass grave. It holds the remains of an estimated five hundred thousand persons who have a striking group marker but no individual ones and for whom annual collective services of remembrance and tribute are held.

The Language of Death

COFFIN

When the King James Version of the Bible was issued in 1611, hardly anyone linked the gear we call a coffin with death. There's only one such reference in the most influential English-language book every published. According to Genesis 50:26 the patriarch Joseph died in Egypt at age 110; "and they embalmed him, and he was put in a coffin." Though the word is derived from a Greek term for "basket," until very recent times a basket or basketlike chest was likely to be used for practically everything except a corpse.

What was the baby Moses put into by his mother? According to an influential English dictionary issued in 1542, the child was entrusted to "a baskette or coffyn made of wyckers or bull rushes, or barke of a tree."

Persons of wealth put their jewels in coffins; grocers twisted bits of paper into wee coffins designed to hold herbs and spices; housewives entrusted the makings of their finest pies to pastry coffins of suitable size and shape.

To a remarkable degree, the language of death and dying is fluid, because persons are forever trying to dull the cutting edge of grief by inventing or adopting new words to take the place of old ones. This helped foster the general adoption of *coffin* as a substitute for the older *casket,* naming a receptacle for the precious body of a dead loved one. Perhaps because many early coffins were made of lead or were lined with that metal, atomic scientists have dubbed a "coffin" the thick-walled lead container in which radioactive materials are transported—no matter what its size or shape may be.

CRYPT

Since the time of the Norman Conquest, Britain has had few long periods of freedom from wars and rumors of wars. Danger of invasion from the Continent or of insurrection within meant that a body buried in an unguarded cemetery might be dug up.

Unknown architects and builders conceived and adopted a bold idea. Many cathedrals and churches were built so that the main floor would cover and protect with stone an underground burial place.

So secure (and fancy) a place of interment obviously deserved a special title derived from classical speech. (English was considered too barbaric a language for use by scholars and scientists; until comparatively recent times no person of reputation would risk it by publishing a book, however original and forceful, in his native language.)

Latin *crypta,* itself adapted from Greek, seemed a suitable and appropriately formal word since it had long ago been used to mean hidden, or concealed, and then the vault in which valuables were hidden. Now more likely to be outside the walls of a church than under its main floor, the crypt for burial is first cousin to the cryptogram, or communication, whose meaning is hidden as cleverly as though it were concealed under the stone floor of a stoutly built abbey.

PYRE

Widespread knowledge of Eastern funeral customs, plus the rapid spread of cremation in this century, has elevated *pyre* to new importance in speech. Borrowed from classical Greek by way of Latin, the term originally indicated any hearth or fireplace. It was easy for the name for such a place of burning to attach to the open-air pile of combustible materials used early for burning of the dead.

Medieval Christians had great veneration for the body as the temple of the soul, so tried when possible to preserve the body in its entirety for use by the soul at the time of the general resurrection. That meant no ordinary person was cremated over a period of many centuries. Burning of convicted witches may have developed partly as an especially fearful punishment, partly because of widespread belief in the cleansing effects of fire.

Even today in the Western world, ordinary persons who know that the funeral pyre is once more in common use are seldom permitted to see it. Almost always, crematon takes place in private. In the United States a stream of natural gas and not a pile of fagots is likely to constitute the pyre. But in other lands, notably India, the funeral pyre in which wood serves as fuel to consume the corpse is an everyday sight.

DIRGE

Because Europeans used Latin as the language of piety as well as of scholarship until modern times, the rites and ceremonies of Christendom long relied entirely upon a language that was already dead in terms of everyday use.

A familiar and frequently used rite, the Office for the Dead, included an antiphon that began "Dirige, Domine, Deus meus, in conspectu Tuo viam meam" (or "Guide, O Lord, my God, my life into thy vision").

Long use converted the first word in the antiphon into a common title for the entire service held for the dead. Once firmly established in common speech, chanting linked with the *dirge* caused that label to be attached to mournful music (vocal as well as instrumental) judged especially suitable for use in time of mourning.

TO EMBALM

Anyone who has ever sung or heard the spiritual that insists upon importance of the fact that "there is a balm in Gilead" is likely to recognize that *balm* may name any aromatic oil or ointment as well as aromatic resinous products of trees.

From the earliest times, many peoples practiced customs that led to such specific acts as the use of sweet spices to anoint the body of Jesus (see Mark 16:1). Impact of this ancient way of caring for a corpse was so great that by the thirteenth century a person (typically a woman) who impregnated a dead body with spices was said to *embalm* mortal remains.

Spices, used theoretically to preserve the body but actually largely to mask odors, were the embalmer's stock in trade until the nineteenth century. A series of discoveries showed that when blood vessels of a corpse are emptied, alcohol (or ether) can be injected as a preservative. Later, tannic acid came into wide use. Not until this century, however, when formaldehyde became generally available and relatively inexpensive were embalmers able to promise genuine preservation of the body rather than mere masking of odors by means of balm.

EULOGY

Until recent times, scholars didn't realize that Jesus and his disciples spoke neither formal Hebrew nor classical Greek. Instead, they used a vernacular now known as Galilean Aramaic. Many words and phrases from this body of speech are embedded in the New Testament.

A New Testament term—often rendered *blessing,* derived from and kin to a classical Greek label for "rendering praise"—helped to shape a Latin expression reserved especially for the kind of praise that is engraved on tombstones. From medieval Latin the much-traveled word entered English as *eulogy.*

Gradually taking the form of a set oration delivered in honor of a deceased person, the eulogy was at first reserved for folk high on the social scale. By the time Samuel Pepys wrote his famous *Diary* at the midpoint of the seventeenth century, he complained that "every body came to me with such eulogys as cannot be expressed."

In spite of similarity in form, there is no relationship between the *elegy* and the eulogy. Originally an adaptation of a name for a flute song, the elegy gained its present association with death through the influence of poems like Thomas Gray's "Elegy Written in a Country Churchyard."

Students at England's Eton College who didn't like being

required to sit through a long eulogy to a deceased professor registered their protest in slang. "Nobody likes to listen to noise made over an eternity-box [coffin]," they said.

Fast losing its influence, the formal eulogy, especially written for reading in word-for-word fashion, seems destined soon to be as rare as terms of praise engraved on tombstones in medieval Latin.

GRAVE

Unlike many terms rooted in classical speech, *grave* is strictly north European in origin. Variants of an expression meaning "to dig" were used by the Goths, by Danes, and by Norsemen. In Old English, the widely used expression took the form *graef*. Because the typical (but not universal) disposition of a corpse required the creation of a hole in the ground, the act of digging gave the grave its name.

Impact of the hoary term is indicated by surviving relatives. An *engraving* was originally a design or a name made by digging into the surface of metal, while a *groove* was a straight line in wood or metal that was produced by digging. *Graven* images, prohibited by the law of Moses and mentioned at least two dozen times in the Old Testament, were produced by craftsmen who dug away gold or silver or copper or wood until a bull (or some other symbol of idolatry) took shape.

In modern industry the *graveyard shift,* which emerged into common speech during World War II, has nothing to do with any form of digging, unless oral traditions about grave-robbing helped to shape it. Commonly beginning at midnight or at two o'clock in the morning, this eight-hour period of work takes its name from the fact that until recent times only ghosts and spirits were abroad at such a time, except for persons who made their living by plundering graves.

HEARSE

Today's motor-driven hearse, though likely to be black, has little in common with the horse-drawn vehicle used in earlier centuries for transportation of the dead. That vehicle, in turn, bore little resemblance to the earliest known type of hearse used by farmers in pre-Christian Britain.

To these folk, a *herse* was a large rake usually triangular in shape, heavy enough to be used as a harrow. Turned upside down with spikes, or fingers, pointing upward, the agricultural device served as the inspiraion for a new liturgical device. Though much smaller than the one used to claw plowed ground smooth in preparation for planting, the hearse used in church services was also triangular, and its

many candle holders looked much like the spikes of the plowman's implement.

At least as early as the twelfth century, the small hearse designed to hold candles and turned upside down was used in tenebrae services during Holy Week. People who saw it so used took a logical next step: larger and more elaborate candle frames of the same sort were just right to place over a casket or bier at the funeral of a noted person.

With spelling of its name standardized in the modern form, the hearse with many candles began to accompany funeral processions to the cemetery. Almost inevitably, the name of the candle holder became associated with the vehicle employed to transport it and the corpse. Gradually, abandonment of funerals in which frames held lighted candles left the name of the ancient agricultural implement firmly embedded in speech to name an internal-combustion funeral coach bearing no resemblance whatever to the ancient farmer's rake.

MORGUE

Paris may be the only modern city directly responsible for contributing a once-technical term that is now in worldwide use to the language of death and dying. From an obscure French term for "haughty superiority," the place in a prison where officers grilled newly admitted persons came to be known as the *morgue*. Supercillious show of authority on the part of officials may have accounted for this development.

It was a natural transition to use the room where prisoners were examined to display and to examine bodies of persons who had died under questionable circumstances. By now firmly entrenched in speech, *morgue* became the official title of a special building in Paris where bodies of suicide and accident victims were taken until released for burial.

By the latter half of the nineteenth century, the technical name had been brought back to the United States by visitors who were impressed with Paris and everything in it. On this side of the Atlantic, any building or room used for postmortem examination or for display of a corpse with the hope of identification took the name of the Paris building.

In the United States, an ordinary death from natural causes doesn't require that a body go to the morgue. But every newspaper office, small or large, has its morgue into which clippings of "dead" (published) stores and articles are placed for possible future resurrection in the name of research.

PALLBEARER

Among both Christians who owe fidelity to Rome and those whose Protestant feelings are strongly antipapal, a woolen vestment worn by many popes has its name perpetuated in the title of a person who helps to move a coffin and corpse to the grave.

Now a narrow band that passes over the shoulders and displays crosses, the ecclesiastical pall (or *pallium*) was once so large that it literally hid the body of the wearer. Hence the royal robe ceremonially placed upon a sovereign at the time of coronation took the same name.

Since the pall, or mantle, served to hide from public view the body of the person for whom it was a symbol of office, it was natural to use its name to designate anything that covered or concealed.

For centuries, a pall, or rectangular cloth covering, was placed over a coffin that was being transported to the cemetery. Four men walked in procession, each holding a corner of the pall. These *pallbearers* were so integral a part of funeral processions that when use of cloth coverings was

THE LANGUAGE OF DEATH   93 abandoned, pallbearers were assigned the duty of transporting the casket (later, the coffin) by strength of hand and arm.

SARCOPHAGUS

During periods when the ancient Greeks habitually buried their dead in vaults or niches or tombs cut from solid rock, it became apparent that various kinds of stone had different long-term effects upon bodies. A distinctive variety of limestone was popularly said to "have an appetite for flesh," because bodies placed in it deteriorated very rapidly.

Once this quality of the special stone, or *sarcophagus,* came to be accepted as a marvelous fact, the stone itself came into great demand for use in making coffins. A body placed in granite might occupy the space for generations, while a corpse laid in sarcophagus was likely to yield to another occupant in relatively short time.

Scholars of the seventeenth century uncovered folklore about the mysterious flesh-eating qualities of sarcophagus. Partly because humans are perpetually revising their vocabulary of death and dying, partly because a Greek word seems to be solemn as well as sonorous, the long-forgotten title for flesh-eating stone was revived and used to label any stone coffin, even of granite or marble, that was sufficiently embellished with carvings to be costly enough to warrant a four-syllable name from a foreign tongue.

SIX FEET UNDER

As a euphemism for "dead and buried," the phrase *six feet under* seems on the surface to have an Elizabethan ring. Actually rooted in burial customs of the past, there is no written record that the expression was used until modern times.

STRANGE FACTS ABOUT DEATH

From the earliest recorded times, the number six has been regarded as important, even potent. As an aftermath of the biblical account of the creation of the world, men were enjoined to follow a pattern of working for six days, then resting (in order to worship) for one day. Beasts seen by John of Patmos in one of his visions had six wings each (see Rev. 4:8), like the seraphim of the Old Testament. King Solomon's great ivory throne has precisely six steps (see I Kings 11), and so on.

Six was so important a number in English thought that a special coin, the sixpence (still considered an omen of good luck that a bride should wear in her shoe), was circulated for centuries. Development of firearms produced the six-shooter (with the number of chambers influenced by age-old importance of the number). Early railway lines had tracks measuring precisely six feet between the rails.

Small wonder that for centuries it was traditional that a grave should be dug in such fashion that the corpse would lie

THE LANGUAGE OF DEATH   95 literally and not symbolically six feet beneath the surface of the ground. There were a few conspicuous exceptions: Shakespeare's body was buried much deeper, to deter grave robbers. But even in an era when few relatives and loved ones bother to measure the depth of a grave, the inherited phrase has acquired new vitality as a way of talking about interment without using the formal language of death and burial.

Last Words

VIOLENT DEPARTURES

For centuries, any person facing execution was expected to deliver at least one choice bit of wisdom before the hangman or the headsman or the members of the firing squad did their work.

England's Newgate Prison, site of many an execution, kept an official calendar on which to record last words of highwaymen, murderers, traitors, and thieves. Often some publisher put out handbills a few hours before a noted lawbreaker was to be executed. Along with authentic last words, such handbills often included "confessions" that many honest folk suspected to come from the hands of prison chaplains.

Logically, perhaps, high-born persons who made sudden and violent departures from the world left behind especially characteristic last words.

James Graham (1612–1650), first marquis of Montrose, was sentenced to death by Parliament, with the suggestion that his limbs be nailed to the gates of four cities. As he proceeded to his execution, Montrose remarked that "he was sorry he had not limbs sufficient to be nailed to all the gates of the cities in Europe," as monuments to his loyalty to the Scottish Covenanters.

Filippo Strozzi, a wealthy Florentine banker who faced death at the hands of the duke of Tuscany, feared that torture on the rack would force him to reveal names of co-conspirators. That led him to decide upon a swift end by means of falling upon his own sword. Before he used the blade to commit suicide, the banker cut with it on the mantle of the chimney a Latin-language line from the poet Virgil. Translated, his last words became an appeal: "Rise some avenger from our blood!"

Marie Antoinette, sentenced to die at the height of the Reign of Terror, went to the guillotine by dark, for authorities feared there might be enough popular sympathy for the deposed queen to trigger a new uprising.

Her final words were deliberately suppressed at the time. Years later they were found in the memoirs of her executioner, Sanson (a member of a hereditary family of executioners who served France for five generations in succession). According to Sanson's notes, the hooded queen refused an offer of guidance as she approached the guillotine: "No, I am, thank Heaven, strong enough to walk that short distance."

Instants later, having knelt to place her head on the block, she cried, "Farewell, my children; I am going to join your father [who had been executed a few months earlier]."

Louis XV of France, husband of Marie Antoinette, is credited with having gone to his death with one short cry, "Apres moi le deluge" ("After me, the deluge"). If the death saying is authentic, it was prophetic, for execution of the monarch plunged France into turmoil so pervasive that citizens of Paris woke up every morning to the rumble of tumbrels (death carts) taking new victims to the guillotine.

SHORT, AND SOMETIMES SWEET

Last words of noted persons are usually (but not always) very brief. In spite of social pressures that have tended to push the dying person or those hovering about his bed toward the serious or the sentimental, brevity is about the only thing such last words have in common.

South African empire builder Cecil Rhodes, "So much to do, so little time."

Swiss psychologist Carl Jung, who did not welcome the coming of death, was attended in his final illness by a housekeeper who gave him stern orders. As death approached, Jung saw the housekeeper leave the room, so gasped to his son: "Quick, help me out of bed before she comes back or she will stop me. I want to look at the sunset."

Napoleon's last words, expectedly military, were confused and all but incoherent. According to a widely accepted version of his death, the conqueror used his last breath to mutter: "Josephine! The army! Command of the army!"

Approaching his executioner who indicated concern that there should be a quick and comfortable death, Sir Walter Raleigh said, "It matters little how the head lieth."

Religious reformer Martin Luther died as he lived, fervent and eloquent in his faith: "Father in heaven, though this body is breaking away from me, and I am departing this life, yet I know that I shall forever be with thee, for no one can pluck me out of thy hand."

John Wesley, founding father of Methodism in all its branches, typically delivered long sermons but settled for a final sentence much briefer than that of Luther's, "The best of all is, God is with us."

In an era when Englishmen were quarreling over translation of the Scripture into their native tongue the earl of Rochester died (1680) with the observation, "The only objection against the Bible is a bad life."

Composer Franz Joseph Haydn (1732–1809) enjoyed royal patronage during much of his career, so called it quits with a fervent exclamation, "God preserve the Emperor!"

Poet Robert Burns, clearly oriented toward more personal matters, whispered to those hovering about his bed, "Don't let that awkward squad fire over my grave!"

Poet John Keats ignored funeral rites and ceremonies altogether and insisted merely, "I feel the daisies growing over me."

On his deathbed as he perceived the end to be very near, François Rabelais held firm to the course he had taken in life by declaring (April 9, 1553): "I am going to seek a great perhaps [sic]. Draw the curtain: the farce is played out."

Noted American clergyman Cotton Mather took an entirely different tack (1728) when he cried with exultation: "Is this dying? Is this all? Is this what I feared when I prayed against a hard death? Oh, I can bear this! I can bear it!"

Jean Jacques Rousseau (July 21, 1778) fixed his final conscious moment on the same phenomenon that later evoked the last words of Carl Jung, "I go to see the sun for the last time."

Convicted traitor John Andre said nothing as he approached the scaffold for his execution in 1780, but as he bent to have the noose fastened about his neck he said, "It will be but a momentary pang."

President Garfield's assassin Charles J. Guiteau, permitted an instant on the scaffold to give mankind a final message (June 30, 1882), cried: "Glory hallelujah! I am going to the Lord! I come! Ready! Go!"

Henry Ward Beecher, greatest pulpit orator of his era, died peacefully in his bed in 1887 but with less enthusiasm than Guiteau. "Now comes the mystery," he observed as he closed his eyes.

John Brown, leader of the U.S. insurrection that keeps his name alive, showed impatience as soon as he mounted the scaffold to be hung: "I am ready at any time. Do not keep me waiting."

Condemned murderer James W. Rodgers (1911–1960) was one of the last persons to die in the United States in front of a firing squad. When the commander of the Utah execution team asked if he had a last request, Rodgers gave a smiling reply: "Why, yes! A bullet-proof vest, please!"

Deeply cynical to the very end, on his deathbed in 1856 Heinrich Heine muttered, "God will forgive me; it is His trade."

Centuries earlier (A.D. 1085) Pope Gregory VII walked off into the sunset on an entirely different course, "I have loved justice and hated iniquity; therefore I die an exile."

In 1823 Marco Bozzaris died insisting, "To die for liberty is a pleasure, not a pain."

Dutch statesman Hugo Grotius, who lived for twenty-four years after a spectacular 1621 escape from life imprisonment as a remonstrant against the power system, was less optimistic, so died declaring, "I have spent my life laboriously doing nothing."

French philosopher Pierre Gassendi (1592–1655) was even more explicit than was Grotius, "I was born without knowing why, I have lived without knowing why, and I am dying without either knowing why or how."

German poet Johann Wolfgang von Goethe (1749–1832) ignored all questions of meaning and of destiny and simply requested, "Macht doch den Fensterladen in Schlafgemach auf, damit mehr Licht herein komme" ("Open the shutters in the bedroom, and let in more light"). (This famous deathbed utterance is commonly reduced to the petition: "Light! More light!")

Condemned to die for his religious views, Archibald, earl of Argyle, was given the traditional opportunity to utter last words after he had mounted the scaffold, so shouted in 1661, "I die not only a Protestant, but with a heart full of hatred of popery, prelacy, and all superstition whatsoever!"

All-time great inventor Thomas Edison, who endorsed no formal religious views, was so convinced that he caught a glimpse of heaven in his final conscious moments that he gasped, "It's very beautiful . . . over there."

Sir Walter Scott simply insisted, "I feel as if I were to be myself again."

Daniel Webster held his last message to three words, "I still live."

HEADS OF STATE

Last words of kings, emperors, presidents, and persons who held the reins of international power during their lifetime have varied almost as widely as those of other noted persons.

Queen Elizabeth I went out with a prayer, "All my possessions for a moment of time!"

England's King Charles II was equally materialistic but more personal when he urged, "Let not poor Nelly [his favorite mistress] starve!"

Dying at the hands of physicians who had literally let him bleed into the great beyond, George Washington uttered just three words, "It is well."

Speaking to Marquise de Maintenon, Louis XIV of France (1715) managed to get off a dying phrase that has become a classic, "J'avais cru plus difficile de mourir" ("I imagined it was more difficult to die").

Germany's Emperor Wilhelm I (1888) refused to acknowledge the presence of death in his sickroom and insisted, "I haven't time now to be tired."

Thomas Jefferson's last sentence was an oral will, "I resign my soul to God, and my daughter to my country."

John Quincy Adams said tersely: "This is the last of earth. I am content."

MILITARY LEADERS

At least as recorded by those who attended them, the last words of military leaders have (sometimes) been mere reflections of their preoccupation with battle during life. Napoleon's injunction to Josephine is perhaps apocryphal, but deathbed utterances of others who devoted their lives to war are well documented.

Dying from a wound received in combat, Lord Nelson (England's greatest naval hero) managed to gasp, "Tell Collingwood to bring the fleet to an anchor!"

William Henry Harrison, propelled into the White House as a result of military victories, survived there for only a few weeks, yet at the end put his last office first: "I wish you to understand the true principles of the Government. I wish them carried out. I ask nothing more."

Aboard the *Chesapeake*, mortally wounded Commander James Lawrence of the U.S. Navy gasped (under British attack) on June 1, 1813, "Tell the men to fire faster and not to give up the ship; fight her till she sinks."

Also dying as a result of wounds received in combat, Confederate strategist General Stonewall Jackson (1863) pled simply, "Let us go over the river, and sit in the shade of the trees."

At the battle of Santiago on July 4, 1898, Captain J. W. Philip of the battleship *Texas* glimpsed victory and death simultaneously, so urged his subordinates: "Don't cheer, boys; the poor devils are dying."

VERSE AND PROSE ALIKE

Especially when they are long and elaborate, written messages of the dying are more likely to have had editorial

STRANGE FACTS ABOUT DEATH

help than are succinct spoken words. Because there have been long periods in which it was a common practice to issue to the public a written message from the hand of the dying notable, a few samples are in order here.

With the end of life in sight, the poet Chaucer is said to have devoted his last moments to composition of a moral ode in which he bade farewell to all human vanities. Though of questionable authenticity, the great writer's last words were long circulated under the title "A balade made by Geffrey Chaucyer upon his dethe-bedde lying in his grete anguysse [anguish]."

Patris, a French poet of a later era, limited himself to two lines:
"Ici tou sont egaux; je ne te dois plus rien;
Je suis sur mon fumier comme toil sur le tien."
"Here all are equal! now thy lot is mine!
I on my dunghill, as thou art on thine."

Italian poet Pietro Metastasio (1698–1782) reputedly demanded pen and paper, in order to spend his last moment scribbling furiously. Verses in which he combined his enthusiasm for both poetry and religion defy adequate translation; with metrical structure missing his last utterance was a fervent prayer: "I offer to thee, O Lord, thine own Son, who already has given the pledge of love, enclosed in this tin emblem. Turn on him thine eyes: ah! behold whom I offer to thee, and then desist, O Lord! if thou canst desist from mercy."

TO BE TAKEN WITH A GRAIN OF SALT

Even though widely printed and reprinted, often in highly reputable reference works, some reputed last words are so lacking in authenticity that they probably belong in the folklore of death and dying.

Philadelphia copper tycoon Benjamin Guggenheim, one of the scores who went to icy death on the "unsinkable" *Titanic,* is said to have come on deck accompanied by his valet as the mighty ship lurched downward. Both men were dressed in evening clothes. Guggenheim reputedly said, "We have dressed in our best and are prepared to go down like gentlemen."

Oscar Wilde, famous for having a finely polished comment for use at just the right moment, became so impoverished that he spent his final years living on money borrowed from friends. According to biographers, his last witticism was, "I am dying beyond my means."

Walking to the place of his execution in 1535, churchman Sir Thomas More (central figure in T. S. Eliot's *Murder in the Cathedral)* allegedly noticed that the scaffold he mounted had been hastily and flimsily built. Broadsides of the era informed the public that the man destined to be canonized as a saint called the attention of his executioner to weakness of the scaffold, then uttered his last sentence, "I pray you, see me up safe—and for my coming down, let me shift for myself!"

Spirits and
the Great Beyond

SPIRITS RETURN TO GRAVES

A common motif in otherwise dissimilar patterns of belief about spirits insists that at regular intervals or in sporadic fashion, spirits return to graves in which bodies they once inhabited are interred.

Dim survivals of this widespread concept are seen in attitudes toward cemeteries. Except for adolescents out on a daring lark, few persons deliberately go into graveyards after dark.

Hottentot tribesmen of southwest Africa have seldom been matched in their ultracautious attitudes toward graves. Until recent times, members of a kraal packed up and moved some distance away any time a member of their group was interred. Distance, they felt, was likely to reduce the danger that the ghost returning to the grave would bring harm to members of the living community.

Growing population plus increasing numbers of graves put an end to mass migration at the time of a death. But tribal magicians still use elaborate rites to appease the ghosts of ancestors and insist upon such reverence toward graves that it is forbidden even to point a finger at a grave lest a ghost be disturbed and angered.

CUTTING THE WIDOWER'S HAIR

Kaingang tribesmen of Brazil never developed a custom comparable to the Anglo-Saxon one of sitting up all night

108

with a corpse. But like early inhabitants of northwestern Europe, Indians of the South American highlands feared that the spirit of a dead person might be reluctant to leave familiar surroundings and quick to return, even after having wandered away.

Men whose wives died were considered to be especially vulnerable. Hence a Kaingang widower went through a purification ceremony whose purpose was unmistakable. Persons skilled in tribal lore formed a special band whose members went to the hut where death had come. They chanted brief lines commanding the bereaved widower to come forth "and be cleansed."

Upon emerging from his hut, the widower was seized so that he could be given a ritualistic haircut. This took place to the accompaniment of chanting that was expected to drive away the spirit of the dead woman.

Locks of the widower were cut short so that he would not be recognized if the spirit of his wife returned. But as an

SPIRITS AND THE GREAT BEYOND 109

extra precaution the disguise of the bereaved tribesman was completed by covering his head with feathers. He wore them day and night until his hair again grew long; by that time, the danger that his dead wife's spirit would return to haunt him was considered to be past.

FELLED BY TABOO

James Cook (1728–1779) began his career as a common seaman in the British navy. His three-year expedition of 1772–75 ranks among the great exploits of modern times. Against enormous obstacles, fever and scurvy among his crew, he lost only one man (who was given proper burial at sea) out of 118.

At one of his frequent stops in the South Sea Islands on his last voyage, members of his crew took wood from a native temple and used it as fuel. Neither Cook nor his men understood when islanders made threatening gestures and shouted: "Taboo! Taboo!"

At least, that's how they understood the Maori word *tapu* whose highly complex meaning centers in the idea "forbidden."

Much that was forbidden was linked directly or indirectly with death. A hut in which a person had died was taboo until given ritual cleansing after a proper lapse of time. A temple, where many rites linked with death took place, was taboo in so potent a sense that any person defiling a temple became taboo as a result.

Small wonder that Captain Cook didn't understand that gestures and shouts of natives were given to warn him that violation of the place where death songs were chanted was sure to bring death to him. During succeeding generations, hosts of anthropologists and sociologists have pondered *taboo* without fully clarifying its meaning and import.

Captain Cook, probably the first European to be held responsible for violation of taboo, very soon afterward became involved in a scuffle with Hawaiian natives over a stolen boat—an incident trivial by comparison with dangers faced on earlier voyages—and was killed. According to medicine men, his breaking of taboo which angers spirits of the dead clearly caused his death.

SEARCH FOR PEACE

Numerous religious systems, notably in India, hold that separation of a spirit from its body does not mean an easy or automatic journey to a final destination. Instead, when good and bad deeds have been weighed, the soul is sent to take up a totally new existence, or reincarnation, in an earthly abode unlike the one just vacated.

For many devout Hindus, the ultimate spiritual goal is escape from the endless round of existence. Buddhists term such a pattern of escape nirvana, from a Sanskrit term meaning "extinction" (as a flame is extinguished when it is abruptly snuffed out). Nirvana is not a place or a mode of spiritual existence, as in the case of the Christian heaven and hell. Instead, it represents deliverance of the spirit from the seemingly endless treadmill it must follow in successive stages of being.

Theosophy, an American-centered cult that blends Buddhism with spiritualism, explains the sudden discovery of a never-before-seen but familiar situation on the basis of reincarnation (see Enigmas of Déjà Vu later). According to Madame Elena Blavatsky (1831–1891), founder of Theosophy, encounter with the unexpectedly familiar involves the soul's memories of experiences in previous existences.

Regardless of shades of interpretation, the basic feature of doctrines of reincarnation is utter pessimism: existence (here and hereafter) is so wretched that the search for peace through annihilation is the ultimate goal of life.

MANY LIVES, MANY ABODES

Orally transmitted religious systems, as well as such sacred writings as the Bhagavad-Gita of India, hold that in the spirit's cycles of reincarnations it may be promoted or demoted at any stage. In practice, this means that transmigration of souls includes the possibility that a spirit will be reborn in nonhuman form as an animal, a plant, or even a demon.

Ibo tribesmen of West Africa hold that if a dead person is buried at the spot where his or her father was interred, the spirit is guaranteed rebirth in the form of a human infant.

Both in Indonesia and in Oceania, there is widespread acceptance of the notion that a spirit may have the good fortune to be reborn as a bird. Borore Indians of Brazil believe that fortunate and particularly holy persons will be reborn as arara birds.

Throughout Europe and the Orient, folk cultures identify the soul with butterflies, doves, ravens, and even owls. Assams of Ethiopia hold that persons whose lives have been evil or futile are likely to be reborn as wood-boring wasps or as hornets.

Among persons who believe that the soul customarily lives many lives in a variety of abodes, religious groups making up far more than half the population of the world today, no other concept of rebirth quite matches that associated with a Tibetan Dalai Lama. Precisely forty-nine days after the death of a Dalai Lama, his spirit is reborn in the body of a male infant. High lamas and nobles who knew the Dalai Lama in his previous existence make a diligent search for the lucky little boy into whom his spirit has passed and through mystical inquiry nearly always find the child!

ENIGMAS OF DÉJÀ VU

One of the oddest of common occurances involves an overwhelming sense of having already experienced something that memory and reason label a first experience. Though sounds, odors, and other impressions are often involved, the most common occurances are visual. From French for "already seen," déjà vu is what psychologists term these enigmas.

A study reported in *Psychiatric Quarterly Supplement* estimates that one person in three has an experience of déjà vu at least once during life. Some persons have many experiences.

Theories seeking to account for déjà vu range all the way from subconscious influence of long-forgotten memories to effects of reincarnation. Though studied intensively during most of this century, no explanation is universally accepted. Havelock Ellis (1839–1939), pondered the riddle for many years and solemnly concluded that "reincarnation is as convincing as any other explanation."

Pioneer Swiss psychiatrist Carl Jung (1875–1961) was greatly influenced toward study of the mind as a result of early experiences of having already seen totally unfamiliar things. At age twelve, Jung recorded a series of incidents that convinced him he was simply reliving a parallel life from the eighteenth century.

Pythagoras, Greek philosopher-mathematician of the sixth century B.C., was once shown a statue of a physician who had lived seven hundred years earlier. Reporting the experience, he wrote that he "recognized the shield of

Euphorbus with a mind splitting shock." Not only had he seen it before, insisted the man who helped to shape the mind of the modern Western world; the shield had belonged to him in an earlier cycle of his spirit's existence.

THREE-DAY RETURN

Traditional Buddhist theology gives great importance to the number three. (So do a great many other systems of thought, including those that produced the Bible.)

Spirits of the dead have long been considered to have visiting rights of a sort, by which they may annually make a three-day return to the world they once inhabited. Known as the festival of Bon, this three-day period falls in the seventh month of the Buddhist year.

Especially in rural districts of Japan, relatives take special care to make returning spirits of ancestors feel comfortable and welcome. After graves have been given their annual cleaning, containers of water along with fresh flowers in bamboo vases are placed on the graves. Sometimes there are food offerings as well: rice plus chopped eggplant, cucumbers, or some delicacy.

Spirits who return for their annual three-day visit to earth are not dreaded or feared. Instead they are eagerly welcomed and treated with generosity and respect. As dusk begins to fall on the third day of Bon, spirits obediently take off for the great beyond, knowing they will be permitted another ceremonial visit home a year in the future.

EDISON'S SEARCH FOR VOICES

Thomas Alva Edison, one-time newsboy who became the world's greatest self-taught inventor, had a long-time interest in matters few biographers so much as mention: the spirit world. About the time his brain was estimated to have a hard cash value of 16 billion dollars, Edison revealed a well-kept secret. He had built and was in the process of refining a unique valve-operated receiving set whose purpose was to capture and magnify messages from the spirit world.

That revelation created a tremendous uproar in the press and in the scientific world. Said editors of *Scientific American* magazine, "When a man of the standing and personality of Edison carried on experiments looking toward communication with the dead, our readers are interested in what he is doing and what he has to say about his theories and his work."

Edison gave a long interview to a writer for the noted scientific journal plus an off-the-cuff report to noted financial expert B. C. Forbes. Neither got any details about his machine. That was characteristic of Edison, who was furtive about all new inventions until they had been patented.

Edison never got a patent on the machine whose functions he had described eleven years before his death. Neither did he publish any messages received by means of it. But he did confide his belief that "all the old and accepted theories" about "the unit of human life" are wrong. Said the Wizard of Menlo Park: "When we find the ultimate unit of life, we shall learn that the journey through far space never could harm it." Personalities embodied in such ultimate units, he told editors of *Scientific American,* "will be able to affect matter [when life in the body has ceased]." To Edison, spirits were neutral—neither good nor bad.

SPIRIT-GUIDED RAIL EMPIRE

Arthur E. Stilwell (1860–1928) built more railroads than any other man of his era—a total of nearly twenty-five hundred miles of double track. He founded forty towns and cities, created a 160-million-dollar financial empire. Charles Schwab, Henry Ford, George Westinghouse, and George Pullman were among those he considered his intimate friends.

Until late in his life, only those close to him knew that he considered most spirits of the dead to be benevolent in disposition and eager to give help to the living. During most of his business career, Stilwell constantly consulted (usually without the aid of a medium) spirit guides whose members he called the Circle.

Born in Rochester, New York, Stilwell quit school at age fifteen and soon left home with about 70 dollars in his pocket. In 1885, urged by the voices that spoke to him from the great beyond, he decided that though he had neither capital nor experience he would build a belt railroad around Kansas City. Success of the Kansas City Belt Line propelled him into the world of high finance.

Acting on guidance of members of the Circle, he bought right of way and constructed hundreds of miles of track for a railroad running south from Kansas City to the Gulf of Mexico. Nearly everything was in order except a Gulf terminal. He considered buying for 3 million dollars the Houston, East and West Texas Railroad (which had a Galveston terminal).

Spirits woke Stilwell from sleep and directed him to the drawing board. He obeyed their instructions to sketch a port and rail terminal on the north bank of Lake Sabine, 7 miles from the Gulf. Port Arthur, the landlocked harbor he built through guidance of spirits, was finished on September 4, 1900. Four days later a tropical hurricane hit Galveston and took five thousand lives, leaving the haven constructed in obedience to "voices" untouched.

O FEARFUL NIGHT

On the surface, there seems to be little in common between present-day observance of Halloween in Christian lands and the observance of Bon in Buddhist lands. But today's Halloween with emphasis upon a trick or a treat by children dressed in sheets and masks is rooted in ancient ideas about eagerness of spirits to get an occasional visit to the land of the living.

Druids of ancient Britain celebrated a primitive All Souls' Day on or around November 1. Often dedicated to the sea god Sama, it was the one day of the entire year in which ghosts returned to their former homes to sit about the fire and enjoy refreshments served by relatives. (There was danger that particularly violent ghosts might appear at any time, but on All Souls' Day the entire population of the spirit world made a trek to the land of the living.)

Partly in an attempt to persuade inhabitants of Britain to abandon heathen customs, in 837 Pope Gregory IV set aside

November 1 as a day for honoring all those saints who do not have a special day in the church calendar. Though the modified observance proved popular and has retained a degree of vitality for centuries, ordinary folk simply shoved the time of mass visitation by ghosts a few hours backward. Hence, All Hallow E'en (or All Souls' Eve) came to be considered the spookiest night of the year. Since no self-respecting ghost would be on the prowl during a day (All Saints' Day, November 1) devoted to Christian rites, spirits of less than saintly nature claimed their freedom at sundown on October 31. For centuries, the living feared physical violence from the dead during those dreadful hours. Gradually, spirits became merely prankish instead of evil, then gave up the night to boys and girls who posed as spirits by assuming bizarre disguises.

PREPARATION FOR GENERAL-RESURRECTION CONCEPT

Christian concepts according to which the spirits of the faithful dead will participate in a general resurrection did not take shape in a vacuum. Though radically different from other beliefs about the ongoing life of the spirit as held by members of other religious groups, then and now, some of the raw materials of the Christian concept gained credence centuries before Jesus was born.

Oxford don Sir James G. Frazer spent much of his life assembling material for a still-monumental sixteen-volume study in magic and religion that he called *The Golden Bough.* As interpreted by Frazer, funeral rites of ancient Egypt helped to construct a foundation for the Christian doctrine of a general resurrection.

Egyptians, says Frazer, devoted eighteen days during the month Khoiak to rites that annually set forth the nature of

STRANGE FACTS ABOUT DEATH

the god Osiris in triple aspect: dead; dismembered with limbs scattered; and finally reconstituted to enter into immortality. Given elaborate ritual burial each year, the god who died and came to life provided a dramatic pledge to Osiris' followers of everlasting life in the realm beyond. Funeral ceremonies performed for dead persons were copied after those dedicated to Osiris (and believed originally to have been performed for him by fellow gods Anubis and Horus).

Early Christians, steeped in Egyptian lore that had been transmitted orally for generations, were ready to accept the idea of a general resurrection, one implication of which is realization that the universe of good, bad, and indifferent spirits has an enormous population—a soul for every man, woman, and child who ever lived.

"THESE BONES SHALL RISE"

In those areas of Christendom where a community dance has been linked with death, propitiation of spirits seems to blend with the motive of dramatizing the affirmation of the Negro spiritual that "these bones shall rise again."

A notable oil painting commonly called "The Dance of Death" and widely attributed to Hans Holbein the Elder (1465?–1524) has preserved what must once have been a common scene in western Europe. Similar paintings of less artistic quality were long painted on town halls, in marketplaces, and in the arcades leading to cemeteries.

By far the most prominent figure in "The Dance of Death" is a skeleton. Dancing vigorously, the skeleton leads a motley assembly of villagers of all ranks and conditions. They follow both his dancing and his slow progress toward the grave.

That such dances actually took place within recent times is

indicated by the fact that several councils of the church found it necessary to interdict the practice of dancing in church-yards.

Whether an actual skeleton (carefully wired) or a symbolic representation of a skeleton was used in community observance of "The Dance of Death," one motive was affirmation that bones committed to the ground do not disappear forever but will, indeed, dance joyfully at the time of the general resurrection of the dead.

WANDERERS IN SPACE

Jean Bodin (1530–1596) is remembered chiefly for his original work as a political philosopher. Like many scholars of his era, his range of interests was very wide (in contrast to present-day specialization). Among other matters that Bodin investigated was the behavior and nature of comets.

Though there are numerous biblical allusions to fiery phenomena in the heavens, the word *comet* does not appear in the King James Version. Influenced more profoundly by secular traditions than by the text of Scripture, early Christians developed an elaborate set of theories. According to some of them, a comet is a ball of fire deliberately hurled from the hand of an angry God, sometimes as punishment.

Not so, argued Jean Bodin in a famous work of 1580 that he called *Demonomanie des sorciers.* Influenced by biblical allusions plus astrology plus numerology, the French scholar boldly asserted that a comet is the disembodied soul of a person condemned by God to wander in space.

A spirit sent hurtling through the heavens in erratic paths, said Bodin, was capable of bringing war, pestilence, or famine. Many persons who didn't accept all of his arguments agreed with him that a malevolent soul moving through the heavens and leaving behind a trail of fire is sent as "a token of the wrath of Heaven" (John Knox). Hugh Latimer, a Protestant who died a martyr's death under England's Queen Mary, couldn't accept the idea that a single soul could produce a comet. A fireball in the heavens, he said, represents a sign of the second coming of Christ, not the return to earth of a spirit being punished by God.

SKELETONS IN TAXIS

Among natives of Madagascar (to whom death is considered merely another step in the journey of life), flowers play an important role in helping to keep spirits sufficiently satisfied with the world beyond to remain there. To these folk, flowers are not enough, however.

At frequent intervals (aproximately once every four or five years, depending upon advice of the family astrologer), members of prosperous families take the skeletons of dead relatives from mortuary casks. New clothing is draped on

the bones, then the skeletons are taken to see the sights of the town in ordinary commercial taxis.

Completion of such a guided tour for the dead doesn't bring rites to an end. Before being returned to its box—with the hope that it has had such fun that its spirit will not trouble the living—a skeleton is usually treated to hit music played by a hired band and regaled by news of the living (delivered in a monotonous chant).

INTERROGATION OF THE SPIRIT

Even though a person has done everything he can before death and is given aid by survivors who provide passage money or pray for his soul, the spirit is not promised automatic entrance into eternal bliss.

Christian thought portrays Peter as guardian of the portals of heaven. Following, of course, divine instructions, it is the role of this heavenly doorkeeper to determine which spirits are admitted and which are turned away.

Mohammedan thought is even more explicit. According to traditions of Islam, the spirit of every dead person is interrogated by two angels: Munkar ("The Unknown") and Nakir ("The Repudiator"). Final exams conducted by Munkar and Nakir take place immediately after burial, while the spirit is still hovering near the body.

Even a deeply pious spirit is in danger of becoming frightened and forgetting the answers when subjected to such a final exam. Hence a long-established burial custom of Islam involves placing into the grave a tablet of stone or clay, inscribed with a condensed version of the creed. A spirit who isn't able to think and answer coherently under the questioning of Munkar and Nakir has only to take the tablet in hand to produce the right answers.

WEIGHED IN THE BALANCES

Verbal tests, prominent in Islamic tradition, are in many parts of the world considered inadequate. Simple forms of the balance scale have apparently been developed independently in many regions and eras. Among the living of ancient times, it was customary to "weigh in the balance" when dealing with precious metals, spices, and other commodities. What could be more logical than to assume that the soul itself is weighed in divine balances and found "not wanting" (see Dan. 5:27).

According to Tibetan thought, Yama (king of truth) presides over a formal hearing as soon as a spirit has passed through the forty-nine days of the intermediate state and is ready to seek union with the Absolute.

At the trial of the spirit, gods serve in the role both of prosecutor and of defense attorney. As arguments proceed, good deeds of the spirit are laid in one pan of the balances while evil deeds are placed in the other. Scales are carefully held by the Monkey-Headed One, who is surrounded by other deities who watch closely to make certain that the act of weighing will be conducted in an impartial manner.

DISGUISED BY A MASK

Burial customs of widely separated peoples prescribe that a special mask be prepared for a corpse and fitted to it before burial. So ancient and so widespread is this practice that anthropologists cannot be absolutely sure why it came into vogue long ago.

Detailed study of remains of a priest-king of the Mayas (buried in a New World pyramid that functioned as both tomb and monument) have yielded some highly suggestive clues. A death mask placed on the corpse of the dead ruler had been made with great care, using about two hundred

SPIRITS AND THE GREAT BEYOND   123

fragments of jade on a stucco base. Wall carvings depicting his triumphs during life clearly revealed that the death mask bore no resemblance to the dead man's face.

Archaeologist Alberto Ruz Lhuillier, who made the notable 1952 discovery, theorized that this mask and multitudes of others in various parts of the world had the same function as the mask of a modern holdup man. That is, it was deliberately designed to conceal features, thereby preventing evil spirits from recognizing the soul of the dead man and tormenting or even capturing him.

COMMUNICATION FROM THE OTHER SIDE

If holy men can guide perplexed spirits and if the burning of a candle can help a spirit reach its destination, logic requires acceptance of the fact that spirits long out of the bodies that once sheltered them can still—somehow—communicate with living persons when circumstances are just right.

It was precisely this line of reasoning that produced the modern movement usually termed "spiritualism."

In the United States, spiritualism was born toward the end of March, 1848. Two girls (aged eight and six) living in Wayne County, New York, reported having heard rappings and a variety of other inexplicable sounds.

Subsequently the Fox sisters worked out a code (1 rap for no, 2 raps for I don't know, and 3 raps for yes) by means of which they posed questions to spirits. Hordes of persons descended upon their rural home; numerous persons of impeccable reputation became convinced that the Fox sisters were, indeed, in constant communication with spirits.

Today it is customary to seek communication from "the other side" with the help of a medium (or sensitive). Many a séance has been conducted by persons who are gifted swindlers; and rewards offered for proof of communication from the dead have never been collected.

Evidence supporting the possibility of paranormal phenomena in which departed spirits are senders and living persons are receivers is sufficiently impressive, however, to persuade many scientists and scholars that this most mysterious of areas is worthy of more investigation even in the space age.

CROSSING THE RIVER

Even after comparatively sturdy boats began to be made and used, rivers constituted enormous barriers to travel in the ancient world. They were major routes for transportation and commerce, of course. But to multitudes of persons during tens of thousands of years, an attempt to cross a major river was a hazardous and costly undertaking.

Small wonder, therefore, that in many parts of the world a flowing stream was conceived as marking the boundary between regions populated by living persons and the shadowy but very real realm of the spirit.

Classical Greek mythology named the Styx the all-important river dividing the world of the flesh from the world of the spirit. Borrowed from Egyptian fables, the name remained prominent in Western literature until modern times. Because the Styx was considered to flow around the infernal regions no less than nine times, any spirit attempting to cross the river was confronted with a formidable task.

At least a few Egyptian leaders who flourished an estimated forty-five hundred years ago intended to take no chances; they left orders that boats were to be buried with them. One such craft made of cedar, relatively undamaged by time, was discovered in a stone-sealed pit near the Great Pyramid in 1954.

Africans living near what was once called the Guinea Coast insist that in order to reach the land of eternal peace, the soul of a dead man must cross three rivers and then climb a mountain.

A perennial puzzle of American history lies in the fact that before his assassination, Abraham Lincoln (who knew nothing of classical mythology) had a recurrent dream of slipping from his body in order to make a difficult crossing of a river.

PASSAGE MONEY PROVIDED

Since ordinary folk couldn't arrange to have cedar boats buried with them, planning for death began to include provision of money with which the spirit could pay for passage over the water. Greeks even gave the ferryman a name: Charon.

Charon's one and only function was that of ferryman to convey spirits across the river Styx to the Elysian fields. Even ferrymen of the spirit world do not work gratis. So it became customary to provide every dead person with "Charon's toll," a special coin of small value. Many such coins were placed in the hands of the dead; especially cautious survivors placed them in the mouths of their departed loved ones so there would be no chance of losing the essential coins.

Until very recent times a similar custom prevailed in Japan (completely isolated from the Western world and its ideas). In order to make certain that a spirit could pay the ferryman for passage into eternity, a bag with a few small coins was attached to the waist of the dead.

Prosperous tribesmen of northern Europe often placed gold coins in the mouths of their dead, a custom believed to have developed independently. Influence of the idea of "passage money" is so strong that in present-day Jutland many fishermen wear a special type of earring. Usually made of precious metal, the ring holds a coin. Attached to its owner, the coin will always be available so that even disaster at sea will not prevent the spirit from having passage money with which to be ferried across the stream that is the boundary of the kingdom of the dead.

HELP FOR THE JOURNEY

Until modern times, typical persons spent their entire lives in a single tent or house. Small wonder that survivors often felt that at death the soul was reluctant to leave familiar surroundings. Since a disembodied soul poses problems or danger to the living, it was natural to provide the soul with help for its journey.

Even today, peasants of rural Poland open doors and windows of a house at the moment a death takes place in it. Sometimes, for good measure, a hole is made in the roof so there will be no danger that the soul will not make its exit.

In Bible lands, burial commonly took place on the day of death. Partly to provide souls with help for their journeys (and simultaneously to make sure that souls wouldn't linger too long), elaborate mourning rituals developed.

Flutes were played, poems were composed and recited, and stylized wails were made—often by professional mourning women. Tears had to be shed in ritual fashion but only at the proper moment (see Mal. 2:13; Matt. 11:17; Luke 7:32).

One effect of such socially endorsed displays of grief was to assure the soul that it would be remembered by the entire community and hence could get out of the place where it formerly lived and begin its journey to the great beyond.

SPIRITS AND THE GREAT BEYOND   127

TRANSITION FOSTERED BY MUSIC

A present-day funeral dirge seems to have little in common with ritualistic wailing (often linked with fasting and with weeping) of biblical times (see Esther 4:3; Jer. 9:19; Rev. 18:19). Both, however, are special kinds of music. These and other types of funeral music have their roots in what were once double motives: consolation of the bereaved plus encouragement for the spirit.

Among the Cuna Indians of Panama, a medicine man is summoned when a person lies dying in his hut. While cleansing the soul by means of fumigation, the medicine man chants a sacred incantation that has been verbally transmitted for centuries. Unless he sings, the spirit will be reluctant to leave the body or will lack enthusiasm about its journey. Simultaneously, relatives gain comfort and strength from the fact that "everything has been done properly."

Partly because it was associated with joyous occasions, partly because it produces both deep and high tones, it was the flute whose notes fostered transition of the spirit from the world of the living to the land of the dead in biblical times (see Jer. 48:36). Even when the instrument used is an organ with many ranks of pipes and when the music comes from the pen of a great composer instead of the head of a simple peasant, any melody used at a time of death derives partly from age-old beliefs that music helps provide the spirit with enthusiasm and energy to get out of the body and get on its way.

AN ALL-IMPORTANT HAIR

Tibetans of Buddhist faith are not so much concerned about the manner and speed with which the soul leaves a house as with its exit from the body.

In order to be sure that no soul is trapped within a body

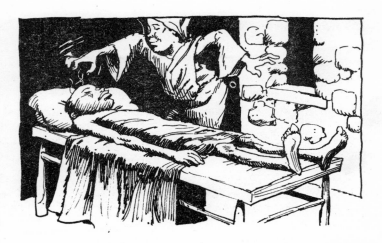

from which life has gone, every effort is made to see that even the simplest peasants get the benefit of a "passing ceremony."

A lama renowned for his virtue and piety is in charge. He sits in the room beside the dying or dead person and requires all others to leave. After a period of meditation, often ended with a brief ritual chant, the holy man selects the "exit hair" of the person whom he attends.

Solemnly plucking this one hair from the scalp, the lama commands the soul to leave the body through the hole left by removal of the all-important hair.

Laymen never perform this ceremony; without proper training and the discipline of a life of dedication, a person might select the wrong hair, and the soul would have no egress. Selection of precisely the right hair to pull from the scalp of one who is already dead or is in the process of dying is so important that for his services the lama receives a gift of an unblemished animal—a sheep, a goat, or, in the case of a person of wealth, even a yak.

SPIRITS AND THE GREAT BEYOND 129

NOURISHMENT FOR THE SOUL

Unlike some peoples who practice cremation as the preferred method of disposing of the dead, Hindus do not place articles of food and supplies of water or wine on the funeral pyre. Though every soul headed for the great beyond needs nourishment for the journey, one liberated from the body for only a few hours is not ready to eat.

Proper performance of a ten-day ceremony means that the soul will gradually acquire a complete spiritual body. It gains a head on the first day (provided that all the age-old observances are kept). Then comes the neck. Heart and back follow on successive days, with navel, genitalia, and anus being formed, respectively, on the fifth and sixth days. Thighs and knees follow, after which the ninth day is spent in waiting. When feet are formed on the tenth day, the spiritual body is ready for travel but is hungry.

To meet the needs of the hungry soul the elaborate and often costly ritual of sraddha (or feast for the dead) is performed. While mourners feast to the notes of hired musicians, portions of food and drink are put aside for the spirit of the departed. Vessels of brass or silver, used in the feast, are presented as gifts to holy men in attendance.

Ordinary persons can afford to feed the soul of a departed loved one only once. Some wealthy Hindus hold sraddhas once a week for the first year after death, then monthly or yearly for an indefinite period on the theory that, like persons, even those souls that have gorged in preparation for their journey get hungry as they walk toward their eternal destination.

MINISTRATIONS AND GUIDANCE

Having left the body and started toward the realm of the spirit, a soul may need spiritual help even more than it needs nourishment.

Among highly developed peoples, natives of Tibet have carried the concept of ministration and guidance to its ultimate. While seeking a path that will lead it to rebirth among the gods, the soul wanders through the vast and many-layered region called Bardo.

Survivors try to scrape up money to keep a priest reading from holy books to the wandering spirit. By listening to the messages so gleaned, the spirit is guided through the dangerous maze that constitutes Bardo.

Always speaking calmly, a veteran lama can sense periods in which the spirit is especially prone to become confused. These periods call for explicit directions which, if heeded, are guaranteed to guide the wandering soul through the most hazardous of regions.

Christianity has no close counterpart to this systematic method of helping a spirit to find the haven it seeks. But during many centuries, the pious have burned innumerable candles with the assurance that their acts of devotion will somehow give aid to and succor the spirits ardently seeking heaven but not yet admitted within its portals.

HADES: A NEVER-NEVER LAND

Numerous religious systems have developed ideas about the great beyond as a place or a region or a state of being that includes potential for real but shadowy existence of the spirit in a relationship that involves neither rewards (such as those now linked with ideas of heaven) nor punishments (like those associated with hell).

In Tibetan thought, for example, the Bardo state is intermediate between death and rebirth. Ancient Hebrews shared with their pagan neighbors a concept of a region, usually considered to be located under the earth (Num.

16:30), in which spirits (or Rephaims) linger without ordinary pleasures or delights.

Sometimes called the ditch (Job 33:18) or the pit (Ps. 28:1), this never-never land of the spirit was most frequently called Sheol (sixty-six times) in the Old Testament. Neither punishment nor torture was linked with Sheol. New Testament writers (heavily influenced by Greek thought) preferred the term *Hades* and attached to it a confusing variety of ideas.

Medieval Christians, for whom Hades was made incredibly vivid by poets and artists, increasingly thought of this shadowy place as a time of testing and of growth on the part of the soul liberated from the body. Many of the offerings made on behalf of the dead and candles burned for them had as their goal the liberation of the soul from Hades so that the eternal delights of heaven might be gained.

PLACE OF PURGING

Purgatory (literally "the place of purging") was never clearly defined by ancient Jews or early Christians. In its developed sense, according to which souls that have gone into the great beyond are required to suffer until having been purged of their sins, the concept is only a few centuries old.

Oral traditions and written commentaries upon the Law of Moses did, in very early times, indicate that during the twelve months after death in which a soul is allowed to visit its body, it spends most of its time in an intermediate state termed "the bosom of Abraham" or "the garden of Eden."

A handful of New Testament references (notably Rev. 6:9–11 and I Peter 3:18–19) gave early Christian commentators a foundation on which to build an enlarged idea of a place or region designed especially for purification of the recently liberated soul. No formal decree on the subject of purgatory

132   STRANGE FACTS ABOUT DEATH

was issued, however, until 1439 by the Council of Florence.

Anti-Roman feelings during and after the Reformation led Protestants to repudiate the entire notion of purgatory. One of the formal Articles of Religion of the Church of England (1562) denounces the concept in unqualified terms: "The Romish Doctrine concerning Purgatory . . . is a fond thing vainly invented, and grounded upon no warranty of Scripture, but rather repugnant to the Word of God."

FIRE, BRIMSTONE, AND ETERNAL THIRST

Unlike Hades and purgatory, hell is a place or a state of being which, once entered, offers no escape. Though the term occurs twenty-one times in the King James Version of the New Testament, the total is deceptive. In nine cases the Greek original is *Hades;* in eight it is *Gehenna;* and in one it is the purely classical *Tartarus.* Homer placed the last-named region as far beneath Hades as Hades is beneath the earth.

It was Gehenna (Greek and Latin form of a Hebrew term naming valley of Hinnom) that put the notions of a fire, brimstone, and eternal thirst into the mainstream of Western thought about everlasting punishment of souls of the wicked.

Ancient Canaanites almost certainly used the valley of Hinnom as a center for rites honoring the god Molech. It was here that children were ceremonially passed through fire, many of them probably having been burned to death for the glory of Molech. Sometimes preserved in its original form and sometimes erroneously translated as "Hades," the name of the place of fiery sacrifice fostered acceptance of hell as a sort of cosmic "fiery furnace" eternally stoked by Satan and his imps.

According to the Koran, holy book of Islam, hell has seven

doors that lead to seven separate divisions of the place of eternal torment. More than any other man it was Italian poet Durante Alighieri (or Dante) who embellished and forever fixed in Western thought the notion of hell as a place of exquisite torture by means of fire. His *Divina Commedia,* begun in 1307, starts with a journey through a most fiery hell that he called "Inferno," a name that still connotes any mighty conflagration.

EXACT CENSUS OF HELL

Theologians of Christian and other faiths have tended to shy away from pronouncements about the ultimate (and everlasting) population of hell. Magicians and devotees of the occult have tended to be less cautious.

According to the *Cabinet of the King of France,* issued about 1581, the empire of the Shades (or hell) includes an immense number of souls who are governed by Satan himself plus 72 infernal princes and 7,405,920 demons.

Other writers of the era who considered any soul consigned to hell to be transformed into a demonic spirit insisted that the exact census figure was 1,758,064,176. They arrived at this total by what to them seemed an entirely logical process of reasoning.

Hell, they said, had 6 legions of demons. Each legion was made up of 66 cohorts. Each cohort included 666 companies, and each company was made up of precisely 6,666 souls—no more and no less.

Epitaphs

ADVANCE PREPARATION

Afraid that survivors would choose wrong emphases or say too much, Thomas Jefferson wrote and carefully revised his own epitaph, in which he carefully avoided any mention of having served as president of the United States. Situated at Monticello, it reads, "Here lies Thomas Jefferson, author of the Declaration of Independence, of the Statute for Religious Freedom in Virginia, and founder of the University of Virginia."

English poet John Gay (who is buried in Westminster Abbey) held his self-written epitaph to a two-line rhymed quip:

> Life is a jest, and all things show it;
> I thought so once and now I know it.

Matthew Prior, a diplomat as well as a poet, penned his own epitaph before his death in 1721. Subsequent discovery of a much older set of lines upon a Scottish tombstone suggests that he may have been guilty of graveyard plagiarism.

MATTHEW PRIOR'S
> Painters and heralds, by your leave,
> Here lie the bones of Matthew Prior,
> The son of Adam and of Eve:—
> Let Bourbon or Nassau go higher!

John Carnagie lies here,
Descended from Adam and Eve;
If any can boast of a pedigree higher,
He will willingly give them leave.

At age 22, in 1728, Benjamin Franklin penned his famous epitaph, in which he used the language of his trade to express ideas about what we now call reincarnation:

The Body of
B. Franklin, Printer;
Like the Cover of an old Book, Its Contents torn out,
And stript of its Lettering and Gilding,
Lies here, Food for Worms.
But the Work shall not be wholly lost:
For it will, as he believ'd appear once more,
In a new & more perfect Edition,
Corrected and Amended By the Author

Benjamin Franklin's world-famous epitaph was not so original as it appears at first look.

John Foster, who set up the first printing press in Boston, struck off a broadside in 1681. Written by the Reverend Joseph Capen, it clearly foreshadowed the famous Franklin epitaph.

Thy body, which no activeness did lack,
Now's laid aside like an old almanac,
But for the present only's out of date;
'Twill have at length a far more active state.
Yea, though with dust thy body soiled be,
Yet at the resurrection we shall see
A fair edition, and of matchless worth,
Free from errata, new in Heaven set forth;
'Tis but a word from God, the great Creator—
It shall be done when he saith *Imprimatur*.

Before Rockford, Illinois, criminal attorney John E. Goembel died at age seventy-nine he stipulated that his tombstone should be inscribed only with his name and a three-word summary of his life, "The Defense Rests."

Goembel's instructions were followed; those of W. C. Fields were not. Facing death in California, far from his native East Coast, Fields asked (without results) that he be permitted to dictate the inscription on his headstone: "On the whole, I would rather be in Philadelphia."

Caught at sea in a violent storm, Princess Margaret of Austria did not expect to survive. So she wrote a capsule biography of her tumultuous career that had included betrothal to Charles VIII of France (who abandoned her) and a formal "arrangement" with the heir to the throne of Spain to whom she was going on the fateful voyage.
Since the ship rode out the storm, the lines she penned aboard it were never actually carved in marble as she had directed.

    Beneath this tomb is high-born Margaret laid,
    Who had two husbands, and yet died a maid.

Long before her death, Catherine the Great of Russia spent days composing and then revising the lines she wanted carved upon her tomb. Courtiers (who didn't follow orders) were instructed to follow her script to the letter, neither adding nor deleting a word or even a punctuation mark.
    Here lies Catherine II. She went to Russia in 1744 to marry Peter III. At the age of fourteen she made a triple resolution to please her husband, [Czarina] Elizabeth and the nation. She neglected nothing to achieve this.
    Eighteen years of ennui and solitude gave her the opportunity to read many books.
    Enthroned in Russia she desired nothing but the best

for her country and tried to procure for her subjects happiness, liberty, and wealth.

She forgave easily and hated no one. Tolerant, undemanding, of a gay disposition, she had a republican spirit and a kind heart.

She made good friends.

Sternhold Oakes, a noted English eccentric, offered a reward for the best epitaph for his own grave. Several poets and writers submitted entries, but the old gentleman thought that all of them flattered him too much. He rejected the entire lot, then triumphantly claimed and received his own prize for lines he wrote himself.

> Here lies the body of Sternhold Oakes,
> Who lived and died like other folks.

TO PART OR NOT TO PART

Traditional marriage vows include pledges to be faithful "until death us do part." Epitaphs prepared by survivors indicate that the end of life may—or may not—mean bringing emotional bonds to an end.

[From St. Philip's Churchyard, Birmingham, England:]

> To the memory of James Baker,
> who died January 27, 1781.
> O cruel Death, how cou'd you be so unkind
> To take him before and leave me behind?
> You should have taken both of us, if either,
> Which would have been more pleasing
> to the survivor.

> CYNTHIA STEVENS
> 1742–1776
> Here lies Cynthia, Stevens' wife,
> She lived six years in calm and strife.

Death came at last and set her free;
I was glad, and so was she.

[In Calvary Cemetery, Chicago]
In memory of
John S——
who
departed this life
Jan. 13, 1859, Aged 28 years.
Cold is my bed, but, oh, I love it,
For colder are all those above it.

[Devonshire, England]
Charity, wife of Gideon Bligh,
Underneath this stone doth lie.
Nought was she e'er known to do
That her husband told her to.

[Burlington, Massachusetts]
Sacred to the memory of Anthony Drake,
Who died for peace and quietness sake;
His wife was constantly scolding and scoffin',
So he sought for repose in a twelve-dollar coffin.

[In the graveyard adjacent to Streatham Church, Surrey,
England, a marker bears witness to virtues of]
ELIZABETH, wife of Major General Hamilton,
who was married near forty-seven years,
and
Never did one thing to disoblige her husband.
She died in 1746.

[A stone erected in Middlebury, Vermont, by a widow]
"Rest in peace"—"Until we meet again"

SACRED TO THE MEMORY OF JARED BATES
Who died August the 6th, 1800.
His widow, aged 24, lives at 7 Elm Street,
Has every qualification for a good wife,
And yearns to be comforted.

[Essex, England]
Here lies the man Richard,
And Mary his wife,
Whose surname was Pritchard:
They lived without strife;
And the reason was plain,—
They abounded in riches,
They had no care or pain,
And his wife wore the breeches.

[Alexandria, Virginia, where James Danner was buried with
his four wives]
An excellent husband was this Mr. Danner,
He lived in a thoroughly honorable manner,
He may have had troubles,
But they burst like bubbles,
He's at peace now with Mary, Jane, Susan, and Hannah.

Milton Bacon, in a CBS network broadcast, vouched for
authenticity of an account of an old Vermont churchyard that
includes a plot with five graves, one in the center and in each
corner. Said Bacon, each of the corner graves is marked by a
marble pedestal surmounted with a carved hand whose
index finger points to the center grave. On each uplifted
hand two words are carved:
OUR HUSBAND

[Bayfield, Mississippi]
Here lies my wife in earthly mould,
Who when she lived did naught but scold.
Peace! wake her not, for now she's still,
She had; but now I have my will.

[Sargentville, Maine]
SACRED TO THE MEMORY
OF ELISHA PHILBROOK AND HIS WIFE SARAH
Beneath these stones do lie,
Back to back, my wife and I!
When the last trumpet the air shall fill,
If she gets up, I'll just lie still.

[Devonshire, England]
Here lies the body of Mary Ford,
Whose soul, we trust, is with the Lord;
But if for hell she's changed this life,
'Tis better than being John Ford's wife.

[near Braintree, Massachusetts]
HERE LIES MARIA BROWN,
wife of Timothy Brown,
aged eighty years
She lived with her husband
for fifty years,
and died in the confident hope
of a better life

[Shutesbury, Massachusetts]
SACRED TO THE MEMORY OF
THE FOUR HUSBANDS OF MISS IVY SAUNDERS
1790   1794   1808   18—
Here lies my husbands, One, Two, Three,
Dumb as men could ever be.
As for my Fourth, well praise be God,

He bides for a little above the sod.
Alex, Ben, Sandy were the first three's names;
And to make things tidy I'll add his—James.

[Horsley Down Church, Cumberland, England]
HERE LIES MY WIFE
All my tears
Cannot bring her back
THEREFORE I WEEP

[From a family plot near Niagara Falls, Ontario, Canada]
Here I lie
between two of the best
women in the world,
MY WIVES
but I have requested my relatives
to tip me a little
toward TILLIE

MEDICAL RECORDS

A special class of epitaphs is made up of those that
summarize medical histories of the deceased. While some
such inscriptions may have come from professionals, others
are clearly the work of amateurs.

[near Nottingham, England]
Beneath these stone repose the bones
of THEODOSIUS GRIM
He took his beer from year to year,
And then the bier took him.

[Plymouth, Massachusetts]
Here lies the bones of Richard Lawton,
Whose death, alas! was strangely brought on.
Trying one day his corns to mow off,
His razor slipped and cut his toe off.

His toe, or rather, what it grew to,
An inflammation quickly flew to.
Which took, alas! to mortifying,
And was the cause of Richard's dying.

[Enosburg, Vermont]
Here Lies the body of our Anna
Done to death by a banana.
It wasn't the fruit that laid her low
But the skin of the thing that made her go.

[near Braintree, Massachusetts]
Neuralgia worked on Mrs. Smith
Till neath the sod it laid her.
She was a worthy Methodist
And served as a crusader.

[Near Williamsport, Pennsylvania, a tombstone illustrated
with a crudely carved figure of a man being kicked by a horse
offers posterity an explanation.]
Sacred to the memory of
HENRY HARRIS,
Born June 27, 1821, of Henry Harris
and Jane, His Wife.
Died on the 4th of May, 1837, by the kick of a colt
in his bowels.
Peaceable and quiet, a friend to
his father and mother, and respected
by all who knew him, and went
to the world where horses don't kick,
where sorrow and weeping is no more

[Medway, Massachusetts]
Beneath this stone, a lump of clay,
Lies Uncle Peter Daniels,

Who too early in the month of May
Took off his winter flannels.

[Canaan, New Hampshire]
SARAH SHUTE
1803–1840
Here lies, cut down like unripe fruit,
The wife of Deacon Amos Shute.
She died of drinking too much coffee,
Anno Dominy eighteen forty.

[Childwall Parish, England]
Here lies me and my three daughters,
Brought here by using Cheltenham waters.
If we had stuck to Epsom salts
We wouldn't be in these here vaults.

[On the monument of a dropsical lady, Bunhill Fields
Burying Ground, England]
Here lies
DAME MARY PAGE
Relict of Sir Gregory Page, Bart.
She departed this life
March 4, 1728
in the 56th year of her age—
In 67 months she was tapped 66 times
and had taken away
240 gallons of water

A LESSON FOR POSTERITY

Especially in the era when perfection of engraving machines
for use with marble and granite made it easy to use many
words on a tombstone at low cost, there was a tendency on
the part of survivors to become both verbose and moralistic.

Many a headstone, therefore, came to include a lesson or warning for posterity.

[Augusta, Maine]
Here, beneath this stone, there lies,
Waiting a summons to the skies,
   The body of SAMUEL JINKING
He was an honest Christian man,
His fault was, he took and then he ran
   Suddenly to drinking
Whoever reads this tablet o'er,
TAKE WARNING NOW—AND DRINK NO MORE

[Tiverton, England, hand carved in 1419]
Hoe hoe who lyes here
'Tis I the goode erle of Devonsheere
With Kate my wyfe to mee full dere
Wee lyved together fyfty-fyve yeare
That wee spent wee had
That wee left was lost
That wee gave wee have

[On the headstone of an early pugilist in Hanslope churchyard near Wolverton, England]
Strong and athletic was my frame
Far away from home I came
And manly fought with Simon Byrnne
Alas! but lived not to return
Reader, take warning by my fate
Unless you rue your case too late
And if you've never fought before
Determine now to fight no more.

[Eastwell Cemetery, Kent, England]
Fear God
Keep the Commandments
and

Don't attempt to climb a tree
For that's what caused the death of me

[Andover, Massachusetts]
JOHN ABBOT, 1793, aet. 90
Grass, smoke, a flower, a vapor, shade, a span,
Serve to illustrate the frail life of man,
And they, who longest live, survive to see
The certainty of death, of life the vanity.

[Falkirk, England]
Here under this sod and under these trees
Is buried the body of Solomon Pease
But here in this hole lies only his pod
HIS SOUL IS SHELLED OUT AND GONE UP TO GOD

[In Boot Hill Cemetery, Dodge City, Kansas, two epitaphs
of nameless drifters warned newcomers of the one-time
boom town]
Played five aces—
Now playing the harp

Shoot-'em-up-Jake
Ran FOR sheriff, 1872
Ran FROM sheriff, 1876
Buried, 1876

[In the churchyard of Bridgford-on-the-Hill, Nottingham-
shire, England, a tombstone from the age of carved
eloquence bears a condensed version of the Puritan work
ethic plus a personal witness by the deceased.]
Sacred to the memory of
JOHN WALKER
the only son of Benjamin and Ann Walker
Engineer and Palisade Maker
died September 23, 1832,
aged 36 years

Farewell, my wife and father dear,
　　No engine powers now do I fear;
My glass is run, my work is done,
　　And now my head lies quiet here.
Tho' many an engine I've set up,
　　And got praise from men;
I made them work on British ground
　　And on the roaring main.

My engine's stopped, my valves are bad,
　　And lies so deep within;
No engineer could here be found
　　To put me new ones in.
But Jesus Christ converted me,
　　And took me up above;
I hope once more to meet once more,
　　And sing redeeming love.

Bibliography

Beliefs and customs linked with death and the afterlife permeate a great many areas of activity. Consequently the literature available is positively staggering in bulk. Only a fraction of the sources consulted in preparation of this volume are listed. Some are rare old books long out of print. Others are standard scholarly studies that are available in most public libraries of any size; these are indicated by asterisks.

Albright, W. F. *The Archaeology of Palestine.* Harmondsworth, Middlesex, England: Penguin Books, Ltd., 1949.

Bibby, Geoffrey. *The Testimony of the Spade.* New York: Knopf, 1956.

Bombaugh, C. C., ed. *Gleanings from the Harvest-fields of Literature.* Baltimore: T. Newton Kurtz, 1869.

Budge, E. A. Wallis. *Amulets and Talismans.* London: Oxford University Press, 1930.

Campbell, Joseph. *The Masks of God.* New York: Viking Press, 1968.

Chambers Book of Days. London, 1869. 2 vols.

Childe, V. Gordon. *Man Makes Himself.* London: C. A. Watts, 1939.

Coblentz, Stanton A. *The Long Road to Humanity.* New York: Thomas Yoseloff, 1959.

Cottrell, Leonard. *The Anvil of Civilization*. New York: New American Library, 1957.

* Cottrell, Leonard. *Wonders of Antiquity*. London: Longmans, Green, Ltd., 1960.

Dawson, Christopher. *Enquiries into Religion and Culture*. New York: Sheed & Ward, 1933.

* DeBurgh, William G. *The Legacy of the Ancient World*. 3rd ed. London: Macdonald & Evans, 1947.

DeLys, Claudia. *A Treasury of American Superstitions*. New York: Philosophical Library, 1948.

* Frazer, James. *The Golden Bough*. New York: Macmillan, 1955. 13 vols.

Glover, Terrot R. *The Ancient World*. Cambridge: The University Press, 1935.

Gray, John. *Archaeology and the Old Testament World*. Camden, N. J.: Thomas Nelson, 1962.

* Hastings, James, ed. *Encyclopedia of Religion and Ethics*. New York: Scribner's, 1908–1927. 12 vols.

* *Interpreter's Dictionary of the Bible*. Nashville: Abingdon, 1962. 4 vols.

D'Israeli, Isaac. *Curiosities of Literature*. New ed. London: Edward Moxon, 1854.

Jones, William. *Credulities Past & Present*. London: Chatto and Windus, 1898.

Knowlson, T. Sharper. *The Origin of Popular Superstitions and Customs*. London: T. Werner Laurie, 1934.

Lewis, Bernard, ed. *Islam and the Arab World*. New York: Knopf, 1976.

Lissner, Ivar. *Man, God, and Magic*. J. Maxwell Brownjohn, trans. New York: Putnam's, 1961.

* Mackay, Charles. *Extraordinary Popular Delusions and the Madness of Crowds*. Boston: L. C. Page, 1932.

Miller, Madeleine S., and J. Lane. *Encyclopedia of Bible Life*. Rev. ed. New York: Harper, 1955.

Muller, Herbert J. *The Uses of the Past*. London: Oxford University Press, 1952.

Myres, Sir John L. *The Dawn of History*. New York: Holt, 1912.

* *New Dictionary of Thoughts*. Rev. by C. N. Catrevas and Jonathan Edwards. New York: Standard, 1944.

Newton, Eric, and Neil, William. *2000 Years of Christian Art*. New York: Harper, 1966.

* Oesterly, W. O. E., and Robinson, T. H. *A History of Israel*. Oxford: Clarendon Press, 1932. 2 vols.

Percy, Reuben, and Sholto. *The Percy Anecdotes*. London: Frederick Warne, n.d. 2 vols.

Petrie, W. Flinders. *Royal Tombs of the First and Second Dynasties*. London: Egyptian Exploration Fund, 1901–1902.

Read, Winwood. *The Martyrdom of Man*. New York: Dutton, 1904.

Rowse, Alfred L. *The Use of History*. London: English Universities Press, 1946.

Scramuzza, Vincent M., and MacKendrick, Paul L. *The Ancient World*. New York: Holt, 1958.

Seltman, Charles. *The Twelve Olympians and Their Guests*. Rev. ed. London: Max Parish, 1956.

Shriner, Charles A. *Wit, Wisdom, and Foibles of the Great*. New York: Funk & Wagnalls, 1918.

* Van Loon, Hendrik W. *The Story of Mankind*. Rev. ed. New York: Liveright, 1951.

Walsh, William S. *Curiosities of Popular Customs*. Philadelphia: Lippincott, 1897.

Walsh, William S. *Handy-book of Curious Information*. Philadelphia: Lippincott, 1913.

———. *Handy-book of Literary Curiosities*. Philadelphia: Lippincott, 1892.

Woldering, Irmgard. *Gods, Men & Pharaohs*. New York: Abrams, 1967.

Woolley, C. Leonard. *Digging Up the Past*. London: Penguin, 1940.

————. *Ur of the Chaldees*. London: Faber & Faber, 1933.

Wright, G. Ernest. *Biblical Archaeology*. Abridged ed. Philadelphia: Westminster Press, 1960.

Index

STRANGE FACTS ABOUT DEATH

Goethe, Johann Wolfgang
  von, 102
Gondola, 78
Graham, James, 97
Grave, 90, 108
Grave, mass, 83
Graveyard, 108
Gray, Thomas, 89
Greeks, 29
Gregory IV, Pope, 117
Gregory VII, Pope, 102
Grotius, Hugo, 102
Ground, holy, 44
Guayaquil, Ecuador, 62
Guggenheim, Benjamin, 106
Guillotine, 98
Guiteau, Charles J., 100

Hair, 128
Haircut, 109
Hallowe'en, 117
Handel, Georg Friedrich, 20
Harrison, William Henry, 104
Hatshepsut, 72
Haydn, Franz Joseph, 100
Hearse, 91
Heart, 42
Heaven, 122, 131
Heine, Heinrich, 101
Helena. *See* St. Helena
Hell, 133-34
Hen, 24
Henry VIII, 19
Herbert, George E. S. M., 59
Hermitage, the, 66
Herodotus, 58
Hindus, 130
Hinnom, 69
Hitler, Adolph, 83
Holbein, Hans, the Elder, 119

Homer, 133
Honey, 49
Horse, 49, 73
Horus, 60

India, 26, 111, 112
Indians; North American, 37,
  41, 50, 75; South American,
  109, 128
Inferno, 134
Innsbruck, Austria, 61

Jackson, Andrew, 66
Jackson, General Stonewall,
  104
Jahan, Shah, 64
James II, 43
Japan, 39, 114
Jar, 54
Jars, Plain of, 55
Jebusites, 69
Jefferson, Thomas, 103, 135
Jericho, 35
Jerusalem, 43
Jesus, 63, 67, 88
Jews, 15, 23
John of Patmos, 95
Jonson, Ben, 45
Joseph, 85
Jung, Carl, 99, 113

Kansas City, Kansas, 116
Keats, John, 100
Kennedy, John F., 17, 23
King James Version, 85, 120
Knox, John, 121
Koran, 133
Koster, Karl, 15

Lama, 129
Lamp, 23